DIVORCE Dirty Tricks

Who Gets the House?

When You Should
Expect Alimony?

What You Should Do
FINANCIALLY
before Filing?

Thousands of Dollars of Legal Know-How

Includes a Checklist
for
Divorce Planning
and
Marital Assets

Fell

Frederick Fell Publishers, Inc.

2131 Hollywood Boulevard, Suite 305
Hollywood, Florida 33020
954-925-5242
e-mail: fellpub@aol.com
Visit our Web site at www.fellpub.com

This publication is designed to provide accurate and authoritative information in regard to the subject matter covered. *This book is not intended to replace the advice and guidance of a trained physician nor is it intended to encourage self-treatment of illness or medical disease. Although the case histories presented are true, all names of patients have been changed.*

Library of Congress Cataloging-in-Publication Data

Frederick Fell, Editors of, -
Divorce Dirty Tricks/ by the Editors of Fell Publishing p. cm.
ISBN 0-88391-147-7 (trade pbk. : alk. paper)
1. Legal. I. Self Help.
GV995.R55 2004
336.342--dc33

200502541

Interior and Cover Design- Chris Hetzer, IATPI

ACKNOWLEDGEMENTS

William Wong, Atty.
For Full review and tireless input

Denise "D2"
For Tireless Transcription

Robert Yee
For his proper perspective...

table of CONTENTS

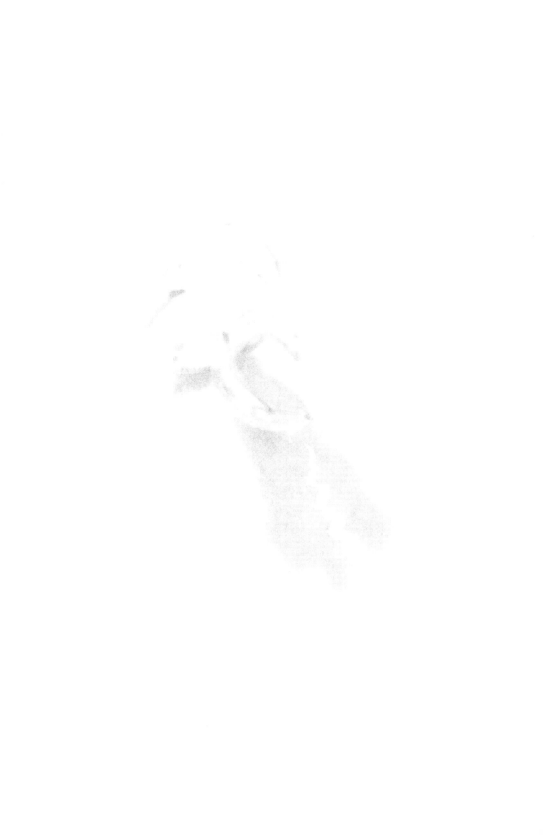

DIVORCE Dirty Tricks

Who Gets the House?

When You Should
Expect Alimony?

What You Should Do
FINANCIALLY
before Filing?

Thousands of Dollars of Legal Know-How

Includes a Checklist
for
Divorce Planning
and
Marital Assets

chapter 1

INTRODUCTION

Not even you can afford to buy so much legal advice about divorce. At rates of more than $100 an hour for a divorce specialist, you need to know everything possible *before* stepping into the lawyer's suite.

A *friendly divorce*, with cheap attorney fees and no fighting, is mostly a mirage. When it's over and done, the elevator ride down lasts longer than the court hearing. But, that's only the climax to one of life's terrible traumas. Getting there in one piece is the real challenge.

Who Needs *Divorce?*

Your divorce status is much like pregnancy: either you are, or you aren't, or you have given it some thought. Even the perfect marriage sits on shaky grounds one day out of the year. Shaky day. Better you should know the ropes, than be caught off-guard, ignorant and vulnerable. Knowledge is power ... and this book will make you smart.

If you aren't already divorced, then the odds are — sad to say — that one day you may be, or you may inherit an *ex-_____* from your spouse, or may have an adult son or daughter who faces *The Big D*. Better you should learn painlessly what others have paid dearly for to learn.

1

What You Need to Know

What you don't know *can* hurt you, particularly if your spouse knows and you don't.

Someone else's horror stories can be the best teachers. These lessons learned are paid for by others. Discover here what others have learned the hard way. Perhaps, you won't make the same mistake ... three times.

Some divorce tricks work while others backfire. If your spouse has a few divorce dirty tricks tucked up the sleeve, better to anticipate the worst than be caught with your defenses down.

Why This is Important

Marriage is the coupling of two people, two estates, and two point five children. Divorce attempts to uncouple all of this.

If marriage is about love, then divorce is mostly about money. Even where children are involved, once the love is gone, divorce gets back to basics — dollars and cents.

Where raw economics are involved, money talks and everything else walks. If you brought the money into the marriage, no doubt you would like to keep it. If your spouse has been the breadwinner, no doubt you still feel you deserve your fair share.

The Right Stuff

Dollars alone do not *win* divorces; the economic upper hand cripples in the face of psychological superiority. This book affords you the psychological and tactical upper hand.

The right attitude in a divorce allows you to attain your goals. Perhaps, you only want your fair share of the assets. Per chance, that includes custody of the children. Possibly, you just want out. In any event, you must sever your emotional ties to succeed in a divorce proceedings. It's a matter of economics: get over the emotion and reduce the battle to dollars and cents. You spouse will do that and, if you don't, you will be the loser.

If you want to succeed, you must be calculating and cold-blooded. No cheap shots. Just business. If your spouse wants to give you everything, take the money and run. Don't stop for a minutes, it will break your stride and you will fall short of the finish line.

Thinking *Down and Dirty*

If you have children, you either want custody or you don't. Some say, "I won ... I didn't get custody." But, if you want custody, then you will need support. Or, when money is needed for your children's benefit, you want to be sure the cash is there.

For some, the problem is alimony. Either getting some or not paying any. A little advance planning can substantially reduce the alimony risk, if not eliminate it.

The Friend of the Court (FOC) can be your enemy or your friend. The FOC deals with issues of custody, support, and alimony. Learn how to make the FOC work as your ally.

Everyone is concerned with property. Learn how to apply this Rule of Thumb: keep what you like; give away no more than you must.

When all is said and done, you may rethink divorce. You may feel it's not worth the price, pack up your toys, and go home. Or, you may dig in your heels, girding your loins for battle. Either way, you will think more clearly about *Divorce — Dirty Tricks*.

chpter 2 **THE DIVORCE DECISION**

Keep Your Ear to the Rail
[So the Train Don't Hit You]

I didn't even see it coming. How many people have said that when "suddenly" their spouse filed for divorce. In fact, there are few instances when the Plaintiff (that is, the person who first files for divorce and sues their spouse) offers no advance clues about what is to happen. Many defendants (that is, those who are first sued by their spouse for divorce) are blind to what is going on, choose to close their eyes, or are into denial about problems in their marriage.

Are there any tell-tale signs that a divorce is imminent? By keeping your ear to the rail, you might predict that the brightness ahead is not really a light at the end of the tunnel; its the divorce train heading straight down the tracks at you.

Where's the Money, Honey?

Money seems to be an early bell-weather about an impending divorce. One spouse begins to hide money from the other, opening bank accounts in another city or not depositing money which routine-ly had gone into the bank. When the cash flow diminishes or is reduced to a trickle, do some investigation.

One husband had two sources of income. For almost 12 months before the divorce was filed, however, he misled his wife into thinking he had but one check coming in the door. Each week, quite dutifully, Mike would turn his check over to his wife and she would religiously deposit it, spending it on household expenses. But Murphy's Rule seemed to be at play: if he brought more money home, she spent it; if he brought home less, she spent that too. It was not that the household expenses were so great, it was just that she spent every last penny she could get her hands on, but could never account for the expenditures.

Not wanting to have all of his assets drained, Mike opened up an account at the Podunk State Bank far from home. He began to deposit his second check by mail into a bank so far away that his less than frugal spouse could imagine. His explanation: because of a cut back in business, Mike had to take a pay cut, as well.

This signal, ignored by his wife, was an early warning sign that this marriage was in trouble. However, since she was able to meet all the family's expenses anyway from the single check he brought home, she tolerated the diminished cash flow — and missed this early warning sign.

Workaholic Spouse

Absence is another early warning sign. Is your spouse away from the house frequently and with unverifiable excuses. You couldn't check the truth of the excuse if you wanted to, such as: "I was in a hauled into an emergency meeting from a sales engineer who came in unexpectedly, then we went out for a beverage."

Prolonged absences by your spouse from the marital home or from the regular activities normally enjoyed in the marital relationship can be indicators. Your spouse may come home later from work, may work longer hours, may work additional days, or may be called "out of town" on business more frequently than before.

Quite often, the increase in working hours is very real. Work can becomes an escape from the undesirable marriage. It may also help generate additional cash for the inevitable economic hardship that divorce will wreck upon the family finances.

A Good Defense is the Best Offense

A change in personal behavior (which indicates that someone may be thinking about *THE BIG D*) calls for a defensive strategy. One important defense is to have duplicate financial records of all important transactions and documents. This helps you value the marital estate.

John didn't have such financial records when his wife of 25 years finally tired of his abusive behavior and alcoholism. Of course, John was too busy swimming inside the bottle to realize that he was being washed up upon the rocky shores of a divorce.

His wife was an accountant. She ran her bookkeeping business from the house. A complete set of files in the basement revealed where the divorce assets had been secreted. Unfortunately, John was not aware enough to know what was in there.

John's physical and alcohol abuse had driven his wife to a decision some years earlier that she would file for divorce. Not uncommonly, Maria waited until the children were grown. However, that didn't stop Maria from implementing a little plan to siphon off marital assets.

Maria's mother lived in Italy. Frequently, Maria would spend less at home, setting aside a little money for Mama in Italy. Maria would collect up enough money to purchase American Express travelers checks and would then mail them to her Mother. Mama opened a bank account with Banco Italiano and, over the years, deposited tens of thousands of dollars in American Express travelers checks which trickled in from America.

During the last five years of the marriage, Maria diverted a substantial amount of money into an Italian bank account in her Mother's name. Risky business, of course, but Maria was willing to take the risk — particularly since she was a cosigner on that Italian bank account, spoke Italian herself, and annually traveled to Italy to spend a few months with Mama in the summers. Maria also was her mother's sole heir under her mother's will.

By the time that Maria was done manipulating the marital resources, she had saved more than $100,000 in her Italian bank account. Given his alcoholism, her husband had absolutely no idea where the money had gone. Maria had managed the family affairs for years and her husband had taken no greater interest, except to turn over his weekly pay check.

After Maria and John were divorced, the assets were split 50-50, except for the extra $100,000 on deposit in Maria's account at Banco Italiano. Maria kept that entirely for herself.   Just a little bonus, or self-imposed justice, for years of suffering through an abusive relationship.

Moral of the Story
Had John made sure that he always took an interest in financial affairs, read the bank statements, and knew where the money was, he might have found himself in a more advantageous posture. Know what the assets are, where the are located, and how much they are worth. If you totally delegate financial affairs to your partner, you will be in a difficult position upon a divorce: it is hard to cut the marital pie ... especially if you can't find the pantry.

No Tellin' Where the Money Goes

One of the causes (or perhaps symptoms) of distressed marriages is the extra-marital affair. More often than not, an extra-marital affair is not the cause of the breakup of a marriage but, rather, it is a signal that the marriage is damaged and that the misbehaving spouse may not care getting caught.

In an otherwise solid marriage, the hopefully rare occurrence of an extra-marital affair, can be an obstacle surmountable. However, in a weak marriage, such frolic and detour signals a careless disregard about when or how the marriage ends.

If your spouse has been involved in an extra-marital affair, you may wish to allege that your spouse has been at *fault* for causing the breakup in the marriage. Yet, sometimes discovering the extra-marital affair is more inadvertent than anything else.

•••••••••••••••••••••••••••••••••

Bill managed all of the finances in his marriage; he was a business executive on an expense account and, frequently, he traveled out of town. His wife Anna remained at home with no children and little to preoccupy herself in her husband's absence.

He may be out of town for a week or ten days and during his absence, she would be instructed to pile all the mail in a big, brown box. Once, in a fit of unrestrained curiosity brought on by boredom, Anna took a healthy peek at her husband's mail.

On the outside, the envelopes didn't suggest that the contents were to be exciting fare. Bills from Visa, MasterCard, American Express, and the like — hardly stimulating reading for a blustery winter night when you are home alone. Anna decided to steam open a few envelopes just to see what the contents might disgorge. In fact, the contents were both interesting and depressing.

The charge card receipts indicated purchases of diamonds which Anna had never seen, floral arrangements at Valentine's Day which had never appeared, and interesting "business trips" to Hawaii during a period when her husband was supposedly on a sales trip to snowy Buffalo. Read together, the charge cards painted a picture of "the other woman."

Anna angrily accepted the notion that her husband Bill had lied while the charge card bills told her the truth. Anna got out the calculator. A total of these errant expenses indicated that more than $25,000 per year had been spent on "the other woman." Anna did some further digging. As it was her account too, she ordered from the charge card companies all of the back statements for the previous five years.

Once Anna had collected up all the credit card statements, she added up $25,000 of marital assets that Mr. Bill had squandered $125,000 on the bimbo over the past five years. It turned out that "the bimbo" was a co-worker and corporate executive. Half of that $25,000 was, by rights, a marital asset that belonged to Anna and not *the other woman*.

In the course of the divorce proceedings, Anna not only got half of the assets that remained in the marriage, but she also obtained half of the marital $25,000 that was spent on *the other woman*. All in all, this amounted to a 60/40 property split in Anna's favor.

Moral of the Story
Read the bills, study the credit cards, and get used to using a calculator because divorce is as much a process of separating lives as it is an exercise in accountancy.

Myth of the *Amiable Divorce*

There is no such thing as an *amiable* divorce. The only candidates for a friendly divorce are couples with no children, no property, and no issues of alimony. Anyone else who tells you that theirs was a compatible divorce ... just told one of the three great lies.

Optimism is at the roots of the myth of a *friendly divorce*. Some well meaning parties to a divorce actually believe that they can terminate a relationship as important as a marriage without stirring up resentments which stimulate financial warfare. Not to say there has never been a friendly divorce. If you believe you are about to experience one of those rare phenomena, then you can only be encouraged to work hard and hope that your anticipated result materializes. The reality is, however, that most divorces are not friendly at all; even those which start out amicably rarely end that way.

The thought that there might be a friendly divorce originates with the naivety of one party. Often, one party believes in their heart of hearts that the marriage can simply be dissolved without having to unload, sort out, restack, and repack the attendant emotional baggage.

When both parties perceive that they can share an amicable divorce, more often than not, one party is experiencing serious denial. Denial is a refusal to admit the obvious. Many divorce participants deny to themselves that "this is really happening to me." The myth of the friendly divorce usually begins to disintegrate when discussions about property settlement get down to dollars and cents. There may have been no bickering about the breakup of the marriage, moving out, or even child custody; however, when it gets down to who shares whose hard-earned pension, or who keeps and for how much, the friendly divorce deteriorates into a predictable squabble.

When a divorce gets too friendly, lights and sirens should sound. The excessively smooth divorce could indicate that someone is taking a ride "to the cleaners." If you get too friendly, you may get cleaned out of house and home in the process.

The friendly divorce occurs when both parties, having been fully honest and forthright as best friends during their relationship, can honestly look each other in the eyes and admit as adults, not as spoiled and selfish children, that the marriage has broken down despite their best efforts. That takes a saint ... or two saints.

The friendly divorce is an attempt to "remain friends" afterward. Those who do manage to "remain friends" usually discover that the divorce was a bad idea in the first place. Not uncommonly, some end up remarrying each other.

A friendly divorce is more of a goal than a reality. Yet, if everyone worked mightily toward an amicable separation of lives and property, that would make you *SMILE* (start making it livable for everyone).

Do-it-Yourself Disaster

Next to the $200 divorce-mill deal, the cheapest divorce is a "do-it-yourself divorce kit. This is a lot like going to the drug store and purchasing a scalpel and a mirror with easy-to-read, instructions for surgically removing your own appendix. Doing a divorce your-self is a very difficult operation. It is very painful, quite similar to groping around a dark surgical theater trying to get the scalpel in exactly the right place. Opps, sorry. It is much more complex than watching *L.A. Law.*

Divorce kits are rarely recommended and only if they meet all of the following criteria:

- *No children* are born of the marriage or adopted during the marriage.

- *No property*, no real estate, neither land or buildings.

- *Short-term marriage* (less than three years in length) and there are no alimony issues.

- *Young couple,* both under 30 years old.

- *No assets* whatsoever accumulated during the course of the marriage; or, all assets are agreeably split up in a fashion that is entirely satisfactory to both parties.

- *No special assets*, such as no pension, or no advanced professional degree during the marriage.

Perhaps one percent of divorces (this is not a verified statistic) involve do-it-yourself kits. These kits are prepared by legal secretaries, some of whom labor under the misbelief that paperwork alone is all there is to dissolving a marriage. There is always the issue of which is the appropriate paperwork. If you meet all the criteria above, a divorce kit might be designed for you. Even then, however, don't be too confident.

●●●●●●●●●●●●●●●●●●●●●●●●●●●●●●●●●●●

David was an insurance salesman who had an associate degree in communication from a community college. He met the above criteria and purchased a do-it-yourself divorce kit.

Before he and Laura had married, David provided the security deposit and has advanced rent payments on an apartment which he and his new wife were to occupy. Laura made all the arrangements for the apartment lease because she was a very efficient woman. She arranged to have the lease prepared and signed, returning it to the landlord with David's check for the security deposit and two months of rent (prepaying the first month and the last month). In addition, she spent the generous $10,000 cash wedding gift from David's parents to outfit their new apartment.

The marriage was brief and ill-conceived. Laura found David tiresome and unstimulating. One day, Laura did *The Vanish*: she packed her bags and left town, leaving David and the newly-furnished apartment behind.

David continued residing at the well-outfitted marital apartment for many months; try as he might, however, he was never able to locate Laura, as she had literally "disappeared from the face of the earth." David decided that he did not need an attorney to get himself a divorce. He paid $90 for a divorce kit and spent 30 minutes reading the do-it-yourself instructions.

David found that he could fill out the forms, pay the filing fee to the county clerk, and file a divorce complaint. After the minimum waiting period (there were no children), David appeared in court and a standard form divorce judgment was entered. As Laura had abandoned the marital home, there were no assets to divide. David kept the apartment, including what remained of its contents.

That was the good news; but there was also some other news. Within a month after the divorce was final, a terrible fire consumed the entire apartment complex. All of David's possessions were destroyed. Remembering that Laura had arranged for an apartment renter's insurance policy, David made a claim on the policy. David soon discovered why do-it-yourself divorce kits were ill-advised.

The insurance company honored the claim and promptly mailed a check to Laura's parents. You see, when Laura applied for the apartment renter's insurance policy, she did not use the new apartment address but, rather, had put down her permanent address — which was then at her parents' home. Laura had named herself as the insured. When David finally uncovered why he had not been paid the proceeds of the insurance policy, he discovered that Laura was the insured and the check was mailed to her parents, payable to Laura. Her parents forwarded the check. By the time the insurance company had gotten around to reporting this fact to David, Laura's parents had forwarded the check to Laura (wherever she may have been), she cashed her check, and the insurance company refused to issue a replacement made payable to David.

David lost the $10,000 worth of furniture in the fire and Laura obtained $10,000 in proceeds which she had never anticipated. The divorce judgment was silent about who was awarded the furniture. David, a proud do-it-yourselfer, didn't know enough to deal with the issue of furniture — since he had possession of these household items, he didn't think it was a subject worth addressing — wrong!

As if adding insult to injury, David also discovered that the lease for the apartment was in Laura's name. When the landlord refunded the security deposit and the last month's rent after the fire, the same thing happened to that check as had occurred with the proceeds of the apartment renter's insurance policy — Laura received her second bonus payment. David's do-it-yourself divorce judgment was also silent on the security deposit issue.

All in all, Laura received some $12,000 in proceeds after the unfortunate fire which had consumed all of David's life possessions. A precious price to pay for a $90 divorce kit.

•••••••••••••••••••••••••••••••••

In another do-it-yourselfer disaster, Norman neglected in his judgment to deal with the life insurance issue. Just before the wedding, Norman had placed his new, young wife on his life insurance policies as his sole beneficiary. Being the thorough fellow that he was, he also placed Rena on his individual retirement account (IRA) as his sole beneficiary. Likewise, Norman named Rena as the beneficiary of his pension plan (which provided for survivor's benefits), certificates of deposit, and 401(k) plan.

The marital union of Norman and Rena was a brief affair, and no assets were accumulated during the course of the marriage. Norman, with one year in law school under his belt, was just smart enough to be dangerous. He obtained a divorce kit, filled out the forms, and since there were no children or real property, Norman got himself a divorce without the advice of counsel.

The standard divorce judgment that Norman used did not contain the traditional clauses extinguishing Rena's interests in Norman's life insurance policies, dower rights, retirement accounts, or the like. In fact, when Norman named Rena as his beneficiary, he only recited her name, never describing her as "his wife." Norman listed the beneficiary as "Rena Steinberg." After Rena and Norman were married,

Rena kept her premarital name of Steinberg. When divorced, Rena retained her premarital name of Steinberg. Now, if you will, several years went by.

In the interim, Norman had remarried, had two children with his second wife, and neglected to take care of the necessary paperwork to change over the beneficiary on his life insurance policies, IRA, 401(k), and pension plan.

Norman died prematurely of coronary artery diseases, though a new, young father. At the funeral, Norman's widow, the now fatherless children, and his ex-wife Rena all attended. Yes, Rena attended, as well. And why not, in the end, she was the beneficiary of all of Norman's liquid assets — despite the divorce.

It mattered not that Norman had remarried because that fact alone, in the state where Norman lived, did not automatically change beneficiaries. If the divorce judgment that Norman had obtained had been more carefully drafted, then Rena's beneficiary rights would have been extinguished by the divorce judgment. However, Norman had misinformed the person who prepared the do-it-yourself disaster kit by saying that there were no assets of the marriage, which, technically, was not true. Norman had done a profoundly poor job of self-diagnosis of his marital-legal problems ... to his children's despair.

Moral of the Story

You get what you pay for with a do-it-yourself divorce kit. Most kits willget you divorced; however, a do-it-yourself divorce kit cannot diagnose legal problems. Without a proper diagnosis, your self-help prescription may not cure the illness. If you insist on a do-it-yourself divorce kit, then appreciate the seriousness of the risk.

Court Shopping

Each divorce case is assigned a judge. Each judge has their own philosophy about divorce issues like support, custody, visitation, and property settlement. Good divorce attorneys know the idiosyncracies of each judge on important divorce issues.

In one divorce, there was a serious issue of fault. The plaintiff (who started the divorce) was an adulterer. When the case was filed, of all the bad luck, the chief judge was assigned to the case. He hated marital infidelity. This judge's reputation was to punish unfaithful spouses by giving them a small share of the assets. The assets were sizeable in this marital estate. The plaintiff's only choice was to throw himself to the lions or withdraw the divorce. To be assured of getting a different judge, the plaintiff voluntarily dismissed that divorce, moved to the next county, and refiled the divorce. The next judge was more favorable to the plaintiff. Lawyers call this *forum shopping*.

Before you can get divorced, you must be a "resident" of a certain state for a minimum period. The minimum time varies from state to state. In some states, the waiting period to establish residency is little more than a matter of weeks (in Nevada and the U.S. Virgin Islands) to 18 months. A few states require the insane to have five years residency; many divorcing couples believe this condition applies to them.

States have established this minimum period of residency to claim some public interest in the division of divorce assets, the awarding of child support, custody of minor children, and alimony.

•••••••••••••••••••••••••••••••••

Sharry and her husband Tyrone had lived in the Big City for many years. The problem was that Tyrone's parents were top level union officials and judicially well-connected. Sharry lacked those same political connections.

Sharry feared that the connections of her relatives may weigh negatively as she filed for a divorce in the circuit courts of that county. She went to a young divorce practitioner who had barely hung his shingle outside of his law offices. He was quite clever, or so he thought. He naively agreed that Sharry's political concerns may be legitimate. "The only way to fight fire is with fire!" he told his client. In order to escape what Sharry perceived to be a political disadvantageous county, the young lawyer advised her to "move" to an adjacent county.

Sharry's trouble was that she did not listen to her lawyer's very specific and particular advice with regard to "moving." The lawyer had advised Sharry that she should pack all of her belongings, find herself a new dwelling, and set up residence there in a new county. With that having been done, Sharry would have been a resident in a different county and eligible to file divorce there. Thus, Sharry could engage in a little "forum shopping."

"Forum shopping" may occur in larger cities where moving to another county might not be all bad under the circumstances. Someone has to move in a divorce, anyway. Since you're going to move as it is, if you feel that the divorce courts where you live are not favorable, given the pressing issues of your case, then you might consider moving. Sharry "moved." Almost, that is.

Sharry's idea of "moving" was to bounce from one friend's apartment to another friend's apartment. She never planted her roots. She never stayed more than a couple of days at one place before she would move on to the next. When she returned to her lawyer (after she had supposedly established residency in a new county), the lawyer neglected to ask and Sharry neglected to tell the details of her supposed "move." Sharry failed to stay in her new county of choice long enough consecutively to establish legal residence.

Assuming that his client had done *exactly* what she had been told, Sharry's attorney filed for her divorce in her "new county of residence." Sharry had represented to her lawyer that she had lived in the new county for the statutorily-required, minimum period of ten days. In fact, Sharry had never stayed in that *new county* for more than three nights in a row.

Indeed, Sharry did move out of her marital home. She moved to county A for a couple of days; she left county A and went back to her marital home for a few more days; she then moved to county B for a few more days before she tired of her new friends and moved back home for one night. She literally bounced around from county to county like a ping-pong ball. When all was said and done, Sharry had not lived anywhere (after leaving the marital home) for more than a few days.

The law required Sharry to establish a "residence" in a new county for a minimum of ten days. Having done that, Sharry was eligible to file for her divorce in that new county. However, Sharry failed to meet the minimum requirements for county residency and let her attorney file for the divorce, incorrectly, in the new county.

It wasn't a matter of days after the divorce was filed and Tyrone was served when Sharry's attorney received a troublesome telephone call. Tyrone's lawyer did not hesitate to immediately inform Sharry's lawyer that he may be in the right church, but was certainly in the wrong pew. Sharry's lawyer was told to dismiss the lawsuit — in no uncertain terms — lest he, Sharry's lawyer, be deemed a co-conspirator in this attempt to fraudulently establish jurisdiction in a new county.

Tyrone's lawyer threatened Sharry's lawyer with an attorney grievance if he did not immediately dismiss the divorce in the new county. Bothered that he had been misled by his client, who had failed to follow his advice to the letter, Sharry's lawyer dismissed the divorce. The next day, Tyrone's attorney filed in Tyrone's county of preference — the place where he lived and where his parents were well-connected with all of the circuit judges. Not that this should make any difference whatsoever ... in a perfect world! But, this is not a perfect world, is it?

19

Sharry was so troubled by the matter that she fired her lawyer and, much to his chagrin, retained the services of new counsel.

<u>*Moral of the Story*</u>
It is one thing to be in the wrong pew, but you had better be in the right church. Be careful playing jurisdictional games and "forum shopping" unless you certainly meet all statutory requirements. If you play that game, play by the rules and be able to prove that you have done so.

●●●●●●●●●●●●●●●●●●●●●●●●●●●●●●●

Mary and George had been married for many years. George was a well know attorney who had practiced before the courts of his county on virtually a daily basis. Mary felt compelled to file for divorce but did not wish to "throw herself to the wolves" — particularly if the "wolves" happen to be her husband George's professional colleagues.

Mary decided to establish residency in a new county one hundred miles away. Far from the sphere of influence of her husband, the new county offered her a more objective and dispassionate forum. The problem was for Mary to establish residency in this new county and to do so beyond a reasonable doubt.

In most states, the establishment of residency, after you have lived in a given county for whatever number of days, weeks, or months that are required by statute, is a matter of intent. To establish *intent*, one must prove a good faith intent to reside in the new county. Now, the issue of intent is question of fact. If one intends to live in a new county, and does so for the length of time required by that state's law, that is usually adequate to establish residency in the new county. But, one should not be contented with mere appearances. Substance should sway over form.

After Mary left George, she not only moved lock, stock, and

barrel to the home of her son in this new county for the statutorily-required, minimum period of time but, also, she gathered proof that she had moved permanently. For example, immediately upon moving, Mary went to the secretary of state's office and changed the address on her driver's license. The secretary of state put a sticker on the back of her driver's license bearing the date when the address change was effective. That offered proof as to the date when Mary moved.

With driver's license in hand, Mary then went to the local municipality and registered to vote. In so doing, she canceled her voter registration at her marital residence and established a new place to vote. Within days, and at the new address of her son's home, Mary received her voter registration card. The voter registration card was dated and that date, combined with the driver's license address change, corroborated when Mary actually changed her residence. These official pieces of paper helped establish objectively that Mary had intended to change her residence.

Having changed her driver's license and voter registration card, Mary then mailed the U.S. Post Office a permanent change of address card. Mary kept a photocopy. That provided her third piece of objective evidence. Within a week, Mary began to receive forwarded mail from the post office which carried a brightly colored sticker on the face of every envelope showing that her mail had been forwarded from her old address to her new address. Mary saved every envelope, all of which contained post marked dates, to show when she had actually changed addresses.

Mary then contacted the telephone company and obtained a new listing and canceled her old listing. She asked the telephone company, so there was no mistake, to confirm this in writing. Not only did Mary receive notification from the telephone company, but she received an envelope from the phone company addressed to her at the new address; the date on the letter from the telephone company was additional evidence.

21

Mary collected up all of this documentary evidence from the secretary of state office, from the voter registration committee, the telephone company, and the U.S. Postal Service. She waited until ten days had passed after the most recent date on the correspondence. In the state where Mary resided, a minimum ten day period of residence was required in a new county before a divorce could be filed in that county. Ten days later, Mary filed for divorce in the new county. She not only intended to reside in the new county, but she had myriad corroborating documents to help prove her intent to change her county of residence.

Having caught her husband off guard, Mary did file for divorce in the new county. There was absolutely nothing her husband could do except to drive one hundred miles to this new county and defend himself there in a county where he and his wife were on a level playing field. It was an unfamiliar court where George had established no automatic status with the circuit judges.

Moral of the Story
When establishing a "new residence," be sure to document your *intent* with plenty of objective, corroborating evidence from third parties. Having done so, your new county of residence can be your forum of choice.

Once the courts of a particular state and county have obtained jurisdiction over a divorce defendant, then that court may make such orders (concerning the care and custody of the minor children of the parties and their suitable maintenance during the pendency of the divorce) as may be proper or necessary for the children's benefit. Thus, even if a defendant is found in a foreign state when a divorce is filed, once the jurisdiction has been obtained over that defendant (even when located elsewhere), then the court has the jurisdiction to address issues affecting the parties' minor children.

The Marriage that Never Was

What if you don't want a divorce? Is there anything that can stop the train?

In most states with "no fault divorce," there is virtually no defense to a divorce. In a place with no-fault divorce, if one spouse tells the court that "the marriage is broken down to the extent that the objects of matrimony have been destroyed and there remains no reasonable likelihood that the marriage can be preserved," customarily a divorce will be granted. In such no-fault states, the only way to stop a divorce from being granted is for the defendant to prove to the court that, indeed, the marriage has not broken down or that there is a reasonable likelihood that the marriage can be preserved. Proving this negative, for all practical purposes, is impossible.

Evidence from a marriage counselor, a treating psychologist or psychiatrist, or other licensed professionals might help establish that a marriage has not broken down; however, it would take a preponderance of the evidence coupled with an extremely conservative judge to stop a divorce from being granted in a "no fault divorce" state. Best advice: don't bother trying.

Annulment

One reaction to a petition for divorce is to claim an annulment. When sued for divorce, the defendant's spouse can file a counter-complaint seeking, instead, an annulment. An annulment means that the marriage is not recognized in the eyes of the law. An annulment is a legal nullity.   Most states permit a marriage to be annulled on the basis of invalidity such as:

- *Consanguinity* or affinity between the parties (they are too closely related).

- *Bigamy* (one party had a living spouse).

- *Insanity* or one party was an idiot (some would suggest that, as a matter of law, applies to all divorces).

- *Incapacity* or too young to legally consent to marriage.

- *Duress* or force (the classic "shotgun wedding").

- *Fraud* (because of some material misrepresentation).

- *Felony conviction* concealed.

- *Drug addition* or alcoholism not disclosed.

- *Impotency* at marriage.

- *Pregnancy* concealed.

The statute of a given state must be read to learn which, if any, of the above reasons can be employed to annul a marriage.

There is an additional requirement to satisfy most annulment petitions: the parties must not have voluntarily cohabited as husband and wife after the basis for the annulment was discovered. Once you discover that your spouse is insane or an idiot, for example, you must no longer engage in sexual relations. Then, you've made your own bed and will have to sleep in it.

The procedure for an annulment is similar to a divorce. If the validity of a marriage is doubted, either party may petition, in the same court where divorces are heard, for annulment. Upon proof of the nullity of the marriage, it is declared void and a nullity.

Many states also have a procedure to affirm a marriage. If there is some doubt about the legal validity of a marriage, a similar petition to affirm or establish the validity of a marriage may be filed.

Crazy as a Loon

Henry had married sweet Marian. It was a second marriage for both parties. Each had grown children and both were beyond childbearing years.

Henry was not unsophisticated, but was hardly Don Juan. His courtship of Marian was short-lived. For six months, Henry would visit Marian at her home where she lived with her daughter. In the evenings, they would sit in the basement, watch television, and talk. From time to time, they would even go so far as to hold hands. Once, they traveled out of town together to visit Marian's relatives across the state. Their relationship was more cordial and friendly than romantically intense or emotionally passionate.

After many months, neither of them being interested in continuing the "dating game," Henry and Marian were united in conjugal bliss.

It wasn't but a matter of months after they wed that Marian began to show signs of emotional instability. She had lived alone for many years with her daughter and was unused to sharing quarters with another adult, let alone a new husband. For Marian, this second marriage was traumatic and Marian felt pressured. She began to see a psychiatrist. When the doctor committed her to an in-patient psychiatric unit, Henry was astonished.

After Marian had been in the hospital for some weeks, Henry was brought into joint counseling with his wife. They began to discuss Marian's psychiatric history. Quite to Henry's surprise, this was not the first in-patient psychiatric hospitalization for Marian. Apparently, she had enjoyed several "good years" immediately prior to marrying Henry. However, from age 18 until six years before she married Henry, she was annually admitted to an in-patient psychiatric unit. She would routinely stay for 28 days for her depression. She was diagnosed as a manic depressive. Henry was shocked. He had no idea.

25

After learning that Marian was less than emotionally stable, Henry had a choice: he could fight or flee! Henry chose not to flee and, instead, stayed with Marian ... for better or for worse ... at least for a while.

Henry's saint-like endurance and faithfulness to his marriage vows was admirable. He remained loyal to his wife and continued to support her in every way he knew how. Nonetheless, Marian still took her annual sojourn to the in-patient psychiatric unit and Henry, without fail, was left behind again.

After eight years, it became clear that Marian was getting emotionally worse and that there was no chance that she would ever be the woman Henry married. Henry petitioned the court for an annulment.

During the eight years of their marriage, Marian did not work while Henry had amassed substantial liquid assets, working many overtime hours in his high-paying, skilled trades position. Henry also kept house, did the cooking, and did laundry and cleaning.

Marian did not respond kindly to the petition for annulment and she insisted, in reply, that she be granted a divorce. Therein, lies the difference.

In an annulment, both parties are returned to their financial condition prior to the marriage and each would be allowed, under normal circumstances, to retain whatever they had earned in their own name during the marriage. In a divorce, however, the assets acquired during the marriage would be divided equally — assuming no fault on either party's part.

Henry countered Marian's divorce complaint by affirmatively defending that she had been at fault in the breakdown of the marriage. Henry argued that Marian had fraudulently concealed her psychiatric condition. Henry argued that he did not know of her manic depression and that Marian neither told him of this mental illness nor did she exhibit any symptoms that would cause a reasonable suitor like Henry to suspect.

There was substantial discovery in the course of these divorce-annulment proceedings. Relatives appeared for depositions, doctors gave testimony, psychiatric records were subpoenaed. In Marian's attempt to take half of the assets accrued during the marriage, she was required to prove that she had disclosed her psychiatric condition to Henry prior to the marriage. The matter was not settled but went to trial. Marian testified on her own behalf.

> **Q.** *Tell me Mame , did you tell you fiancé, that you were suffering from manic depressive illness?*
>
> **A.** *Of course, he knew that I wasn't well. He could see my purse. He had to know I was taking medication. Any fool would know those weren't aspirin I was taking. If he didn't know, he sure was stupid!*
>
> **Q.** *But, my question is this: did your husband know, before you were married, that you were seeing a psychiatrist to treat for a mental illness?*
>
> **A.** *He knew. He knew I was seeing a doctor. How could he not know? He dropped me off every Thursday. He had to know it was a psychiatrist. That medical building was just full of psychiatrists. If he didn't know, then he really must have been blind as a bat.*

Henry agreed that he knew that Marian had taken pills but he had absolutely no idea what the pills were for. In fact, he didn't even seem curious why she was taking pills. He never asked her because he innocently believed it was "none of his business."

No doubt, Henry drove Marian to her weekly sessions, but he did not know what kind of doctor she was seeing. Both Henry and Marian were basic, honest people. Henry's testimony was quite credible.

The ultimate proof, which weighed heavily in favor of Henry, was the testimony of Marian's psychiatrist.

> **Q.** *Doctor, what do you recall about Marian's decision about whether or not to tell her prospective husband about her mental illness?*
>
> **A.** *I distinctly remember the group therapy session before Marian accepted Henry's marriage proposal. The group was composed entirely of women who shared Marian's manic depressive condition.*
>
> **Q.** *Did any of these women offer any advice to Marian about disclosing her mental illness?*
>
> **A.** *One woman in the therapy group stated, 'I don't think you should tell him anything, Marian. He has no right to know. You've had six good years with out hospitalization. What he doesn't know won't hurt him. Your mental condition is your business.' It was that attitude which prevailed in the group therapy session.*
>
> **Q.** *What did you advise Marian, if anything, about full disclosure to her soon-to-be husband?*
>
> **A.** *I advised Marian to be candid with her fiancé. Instead, she disregarded my advice and took her guidance from the other women in her therapy group.*

It was clear from the testimony that Marian had concealed a

material condition about her mental health. Even though Henry had continued to reside with Marian, as husband and wife, after he obtained actual knowledge of this fraud, the judge did not require a 50/50 split of all of the marital assets.

In the end, Marian left the marriage with every asset she had brought in, as did Henry; Henry paid Marian about one-third of the marital assets that had been acquired during their eight year marriage.

Moral of the Story

If you continue marital relations with your spouse — once you have grounds for annulment — you may have waived your right to complain. If you want to get out of the marriage, leave while the gettin' is good. As soon as you learn the bad news, it's leave it, or love it. If you hesitate, you may lose the right to an annulment.

Abandonment

A simple basis for divorce is abandonment. In some common law countries, abandonment is the easy way out of a marriage. To qualify, one spouse must have completely abandoned or be separated from the other without permission for a minimum period. That minimum period of abandonment or separation can range from 18 months to 10 years, though usually is one or two years.

Those who are abandoned normally retain all the property in their possession. These divorces are routine, except that the other spouse is normally notified by publication. That is, a newspaper will publish the filing of the divorce complaint for a number of weeks. If the disappearing spouse does not answer the "want ad," the divorced is granted as requested.

Separate But Equal

An alternative to divorce or annulment is an action for separate maintenance. Separate maintenance is sometimes called a "divorce from bed and board." Under a separate maintenance decree, the parties remain married for all legal purposes, yet the court divides the property. There are often some good reasons to prefer separation instead of divorce.

Religious objections may provide reasons for separate maintenance, particularly where there are religious objections to divorce. In the Catholic church, for example, divorced Catholics — while welcomed to participate in church services — are forbidden from receiving the sacraments. To those who keep this faith, a divorce might be abhorrent, while a separation is a tolerable alternative if there is no immediate intent to be remarried. If remarriage becomes possible, then a divorce can be filed and readily obtained much more simply (because property has already been divided).

Senior citizens may seek separate maintenance for reasons of financial security. For some, children and relatives might place undue pressure on older parents not to be divorced. In these circumstances, a separate maintenance decree might be relatively more palatable.

Pension options may dictate a preference for separate maintenance, such as pension programs which provide surviving spouse options. Upon divorce, the "surviving spouse option" under a pension agreement becomes inoperative. Thus, if an older couple were to divorce, once the pension recipient dies, the surviving spouse receives no benefit. Some pension recipients choose not to be divorced but, rather, elect to remain legally married (though separated by a decree of the court); this enables the surviving spouse to enjoy pension benefits.

Hospitalization insurance is another reason to prefer separation over divorce. Some retirement plans provide for hospitalization insurance for a "retiree and spouse." Where these benefits are available, which are very expensive outside of a group health insurance plan, divorce can mean paying several thousands of dollars a year for the divorced spouse. Under a separate maintenance decree, all personal property can be divided and the legality of the marriage is preserved; this allows both the spouse and the retiree to continue this health care coverage, and realize the benefits of a "divorce from bed and board."

Social Security options may dictate a preference for separate maintenance. The Social Security Administration, after 20 years of marriage, allows a non-working spouse to collect social security benefits of the working spouse who had since died. Where parties are close to reaching the 20 year mark, it may be important to be separated, remaining legally married, until after the 20 year mark has been passed.

Hoping to preserve a marriage, some prefer separate maintenance rather than divorce. The breakdown in the marriage may have been so severe that the objects of matrimony may have been destroyed; however, there may still remain a reasonable likelihood that the marriage can be preserved.

•••••••••••••••••••••••••••••••••••

Sam and Mary had each been previously married. The children of each couple were, to a person, uniformly opposed to this second marriage. It was not the couple who caused their own breakdown but, rather, their inability to deal with their children's non-acceptance of the marriage.

During a particularly traumatic summer vacation, Sam and Mary vacationed at Sam's family cottage. His children, used to seeing their father with their now-deceased mother, objected to this second marriage. Perhaps, in the opinion of Sam's children, he had married too soon. He thought that was his business, not theirs. Family dissent over-shadowed the summer holidays rather than familial bliss.

The tension of the summer increased and finally exploded by Labor Day. By then, neither Mary nor Sam were speaking with each other. They had packed their personal belongings and headed back toward their condominium in town.

The anger that had boiled over during the summer continued simmering as the new year approached. By the year's end, Sam and Mary were not even exchanging a "How do you do?"

After the seasonal holidays, Sam came to his attorney begging for a divorce. Mary counter-claimed the complaint for divorce by seeking a decree of separate maintenance. The couple talked about the benefits of avoiding a divorce, hoping to preserve the marriage, though neither was optimistic. Both had endured such trauma during the preceding half year and the wounds were still rather raw, however, their marriage was still quite young. They decided to divide the marital assets equally, each taking from the marriage what they had brought in.

Rather than getting divorced, they chose to remain married, entering a decree of separate maintenance. An interesting feature was included in the separate maintenance decree: both were required to attend marriage counseling until or unless such time as the marriage counselor and the couple agreed that counseling was fruitless and the marriage could not be preserved.

A year later, both continued to go to marriage counseling and continued to see each other socially, to the exclusion of others. Whether a separate maintenance decree can preserve that marriage, remains to be seen, but a creative effort was made toward that end.

<u>*Moral of the Story*</u>
If you can't bring yourself to be divorced, or if divorce is to you economic disadvantage, and both of you agree, a decree of separate maintenance may offer an alternative.

Prenuptial Agreements

Those who have been ground into hamburger by a previous, messy divorce will consider a pre-nuptial agreement. While these contracts are honored in some states, other state courts have not yet ruled on their validity.

There are some basic requirements when you attempt to draft a pre-nuptial agreement which will improve the odds that it will be upheld by a judge if need be. Some states disallow pre-nuptial agreements because they are made "in contemplation of divorce." That does not mean, however, that one cannot execute a pre-nuptial agreement which might contemplate, among other things, divorce, annulment, separation, death, disability, or other exigent circumstances. Combining multiple purposes increases the possibility that a pre-nuptial might be honored by a court.

Full disclosure of assets is one essential to a pre-nuptial agreement. Both parties must enter the agreement fully appreciating the extent of their own wealth and disclosing that, as well as being fully aware of the wealth of their spouse. Such awareness means that you not only must know the nature and extent of your respective bounty but, also, you must be appraised of the fair value of each of these assets. Full disclosure being made, each of the parties to such an agreement is better able to make an intelligent decision as to whether or not to enter into such a contract.

Separate and independent counsel for each party is imperative. This two-fold test is important: each party must have separate counsel to advise them as to whether or not they should enter into such an agreement and as to their options, under the circumstances; additionally, the attorneys representing each party must be independent of each other. Therefore, attorneys from the same firm can hardly offer independent counsel to both parties under most circumstances.

Fair distribution of wealth accumulated during the marriage is a critical element. Pre-nuptial agreements may return each party to their financial condition before the marriage; however, the courts like some monetary recognition for wealth accumulated during the marriage. The parties need not share equally in every dollar that accrues during the marriage; however, there must be some payment to the spouse who is less financially well off. A spouse might be awarded a certain number of dollars for each year that they are married before death, disability, divorce, separation, or annulment occurs.

In reality, few engaged couples enter into pre-nuptial agreements. For most, discussion of finances, particularly in contemplation of divorce, is so uncomfortable that nearly everyone avoids the discussion. Some parties, however, who have accumulated wealth before marriage, place their assets in a trust, beyond the reach of most divorce courts. Thus, there are no assets brought into the marriage because everything is in a trust.

••••••••••••••••••••••••••••••••••

Maria and Chuck were to be married. Both had been professionals for many years prior to the wedding. However, Chuck required that Maria quit her job many states away and move to where he was located. That was in the best interest of Chuck's career. Maria did just that, incurring not only a substantial moving expense to accommodate her fiancé but, also, suffering a serious cut in pay to take a new job in Chuck's city where she was to be married.

Some weeks before the wedding, Chuck suggested that he and Maria visit Chuck's attorney to discuss a pre-nuptial agreement. Chuck, having been previously married, was still stinging from having divided his assets once before in a divorce. He wanted to be sure that the same financial fate would not befall him again. Willing to do almost anything for her fiancé, Maria accommodated Chuck. they visited Chuck's corporate lawyer some days prior to the wedding.

Unfamiliar with pre-nuptial agreements, this corporate attorney drafted a contract. He advised both Maria and Chuck as to the implications, but made no effort to review Chuck's tax returns or personal financial statements to determine that Chuck had fully disclosed all assets. Inadvertently, (or, maybe, deliberately) Chuck had not disclosed two obscure brokerage accounts which comprised the lion's share of his liquid assets. Chuck's attorney did not insist that Maria seek the opinion of outside legal counsel but, rather, made the mistake of advising both parties as if they were one client.

Some years later, Maria sued Chuck for divorce. He produced, in his own defense, this pre-nuptial agreement. Nonetheless, Maria demanded an equal division of the assets, regardless of the pre-nuptial agreement. Maria successfully argued that she had sacrificed a good professional position to relocate to the city where Chuck lived and did so at some substantial personal expense. Chuck also had failed to disclose all of his assets. While taking Maria to his own business attorney, he deprived Maria of independent legal counsel. For all of these reasons, the court refused to uphold the pre-nuptial agreement which, if care had been taken, would have guided the property settlement.

Moral of the Story
If you're going to do it (that is, a pre-nuptial agreement), do it right! Have independent legal counsel for each party to a pre-nuptial agreement review tax returns for five years before the agreement is signed. Disclose all assets.

Make provision for the fair distribution of assets accumulated during the marriage. Don't call the document a "Pre-Nuptial Agreement" but, rather, entitle it an "Asset Distribution Agreement." This will encourage the court to uphold the agreement, but there is no guarantee that it will be rigidly followed. Regardless, it can't hurt to have a pre-nuptial agreement and will probably help if it is your assets at stake. Better than a pre-nuptial agreement, consider a trust.

Divorce Spending Sprees

One way some parties help themselves to a few extra marital assets is to engage in a divorce spending spree. These bouts of financial recklessness usually occur just about the time when the divorce complaint is filed, before a judge can put a stop to this financial hemorrhaging.

Rose and Calvin were married for a short time. It was a whirl-wind romance and a marriage which occurred too quickly. Rose had decided that, in exchange for her having married Calvin so willingly, on the way out the door she would help herself to a few goodies ... at Calvin's expense, of course.

Calvin had generously given Rose two credit cards, with the explicit understanding that these were to be used for marital expenses only. Rose had something else in mind before deserting Calvin. Rose went to some of the finer clothing stores and acquired a wonderful spring and summer wardrobe. When she reached the maximum credit limit on the first credit card, she began the same process anew with the second piece of plastic. Having run both credit cards to their limits, she carefully packaged everything away and was discrete enough not to flaunt it in Calvin's face. But it wasn't enough to have a new wardrobe unless you had someplace to go—and somehow to get there.

Rose began to pester Calvin about the tiny apartment that they lived in. Rose had absolutely no credit history and, standing alone, could borrow no cash. Rose took Calvin mobile-home hunting one day. She persuaded Calvin that if they take two mobile homes, join them together, and add a few extras, for a mere $60,000 in total, they would have an instant starter home. All that would be required is a $12,000 down payment and they would be in the "driver's seat," with a brand new mobile home. Rose really did anticipate being in the "driver's seat," but she did not intend that she and Calvin would be in it together.

Calvin borrowed one-half of in his retirement plan (which would have given him the full $60,000) at a remarkably low interest rate. This would allow Rose and Calvin to pay cash for their new mobile home and, at a low interest rate, slowly repay Calvin's pension plan. Calvin deposited the $60,000 into a joint account, from which money could be withdrawn by either Rose or himself. Rose scheduled an appointment the following weekend to select their dream mobile home. The next Friday, Rose disappeared. Needless to say, the following week was frantic for Calvin, not knowing Rose's whereabouts.

It was after one week that Calvin discovered the bank account (into which he had deposited the $60,000 to purchase the mobile home) was quite empty. The entire $60,000 had been withdrawn on the Friday of Rose's disappearance and a cashier's check had been made payable to a local Mercedes Benz dealer. Apparently, Calvin's wife was no longer a "second-hand Rose" as she was now driving a brand new Mercedes Benz and heading somewhere far away, never to see Calvin again.

Rose was never seen, despite her wonderful new summer wardrobe and fully paid-for Mercedes Benz. Calvin got divorced, got to pay off both credit cards which he had so generously given to his wife, and never got a chance to drive the Mercedes Benz.

Moral of the Story
Have good reasons to place full faith and credit in your spouse, both from a character and financial standpoint. Don't be too eager to demonstrate your love by reckless financial behavior. Be as good of a judge of character with your spouse as with any business "partner."

Cutting Up the Credit Cards

Divorce spending sprees are often fueled by joint credit cards just after a divorce has been filed. An abandoned spouse may be righteously indignant over being named as the defendant in an unwanted divorce proceeding. The natural, human tendency for revenge can be overwhelming once served with divorce papers. Some spouses take it upon themselves to level the financial playing field. Andrea was such a spouse.

The divorce had been several years in the making. Karl had been secretly involved with another woman for years before he filed for divorce from Andrea. Karl had been somewhat discrete but, in a moment of intentional or unintentional carelessness, had left lying about a collection of account statements from one of his credit cards. Andrea found these credit card statements and persistently noticed the name of a ill-reputed topless bar called "Jason's Place." As Andrea leafed through the collection of credit card statements, it didn't take a rocket scientist to figure that Karl had spent as much as $10,000 at Jason's Place over the last several years.

A certain type of woman, sometimes called an "independent contractor," worked at Jason's. In fact, these "independent contractors" paid the bar owner for the privilege of working at Jason's. The topless (and practically bottomless) bar maids earned generous tips from the businessmen clientele. This place of employment offered fertile ground for after-hours "dates." Karl had frequented Jason's Place but, carelessly, had left behind a trail of his deceit and imprudence.

Andrea decided that she would level the financial playing field. She had several of Karl's credit cards, in his name alone, with credit limits which were not fully tapped.

Andrea took each credit card and, in turn, exercised it to the maximum potential. Unilaterally, Andrea awarded herself, after the divorce was filed, a new wardrobe, a down-payment on a new car, plus a spate of cash advances which she used to acquire every new thing that she had long been denied. During Karl's period of infidelity, Andrea had scrimped and saved, socked away pennies, and made the household hum on little cash. Having discovered her husband's mistress, Andrea helped herself to a little booty in advance of the divorce trial.

By the time this divorce was ready for trial, Andrea had uncovered an entire trail of Karl's misexpenditures. Andrea had so quickly run all of his credit cards to the maximum — for things which were absolutely necessary in light of Karl's financial abandonment in her time of need — that she had totally reoutfitted her life.

Since Karl had been freely spending joint marital assets on his trysts, Andrea was awarded all of the goods and services that she had advanced herself on Karl's credit cards; in turn, as punishment for his indiscretion, Karl was awarded the debts associated with these credit cards.

Moral of the Story
Give your spouse no access to lines of credit, credit cards, or other liquid asset accounts that any angry spouse can use against as economic punishment.

Reeling in the Lines of Credit

When filing for divorce, close all joint credit accounts and destroy all credit cards for which you may be liable. Get physical possession of all such credit cards that have your name on them. But that alone, is not enough.

Additionally, you must also inform the credit card company that these credit cards are now "missing." You should ask the credit card company to cancel those account numbers.

Some people are reluctant to actually take physical possession of joint credit cards and credit cards in their own name. Those who hesitate, lose. If you anticipate filing for divorce, there is no better advice you can act upon than to wait until your spouse is in the shower, and take all credit cards into your possession and destroy them. Discuss it later, but do it now.

Call the credit card company immediately and report that your credit cards are "missing." Ask that all present accounts be canceled. Advise the credit card company immediately and in writing of your new address (perhaps a post office box, your business, or some secure location where your spouse has no access). Ask that a new credit card (but only for credit cards in your name alone) be issued and mailed to your new address.

Do not reopen any joint accounts in the name of both spouses, even with a new account number. Your spouse may discover the existence of the new account number and can arrange to receive one of the newly-issued cards. Mistakes happen all the time. You can't count on the credit card company to do what you told them to do.

If you fail to destroy joint credit cards and cancel those accounts, you may live to regret it — or at least live to pay off the balance due which, if not paid in full and timely, will poorly affect your credit rating.

Robbing the Bank

Before filing for a divorce, you need to identify all liquid assets. A liquid asset is a savings account, checking account, brokerage account, and any other form of money that can easily be converted to cash. Once you have identified all liquid assets, you should determine whether or not to take control of these assets. Often, the first advice an attorney gives is to break the bank and personally seize all liquid assets, closing out accounts, and opening a new account. Know this: if you don't do it, your spouse will.

When you break the bank, you could equitably divide all of the assets by taking exactly one-half of every liquid asset account. That leaves the remainder for your spouse and no one can quibble about getting less than half of the cash on hand. The second approach is to take control and seize all of the liquid assets and to place them into your sole name as protection. Do this if your spouse should fail to keep enough money on hand to pay debts or obligations (for which you might be jointly obligated and for which your credit standing is at risk).

The safest approach is to withdraw at least one-half of the

assets. However, if there are many joint marital debts and if you are afraid that they might not be paid in full — risking your credit worthiness — then you might consider paying off all joint debts with the joint cash on hand, equally splitting the net amount which remains.

These are complicated matters and decisions should not be made in a vacuum. Before unilaterally making any decision about assets, consult an attorney. But do so before the divorce complaint is filed and follow your lawyer's advice.

Stealing the Family Records

One vital commodity in divorces with substantial assets is the financial records. There is a tremendous advantage to be in possession of the financial records of a marriage. Woe be to those who neither have the records, nor understand them where substantial assets are at stake.

Some spouses take little or no interest in the financial affairs of the marriage. They relegate it to their partner to make decisions regarding financial matters and to handle monetary affairs. This may be well and good during a solid marriage where each party takes responsibility for their respective duties; however, should a divorce confront the financially ignorant spouse, the economic impact can be crippling where deceit is afoot.

Make a list of assets. Know each asset that you have and where it is located. Some clients, beyond knowing that they have a home and a car, could not even begin to list the variety of financial accounts or brokerage institutions where their liquid assets are maintained.

Besides wanting to know what the assets are, you must know the value of those assets. You will need to produce documentation for values, preferably the most recent statement and statements for the last five years. You should also locate tax returns and remember that check registers are important, particularly where a deceitful spouse may have been siphoning off marital assets, hiding them in anticipation of divorce.

•••••••••••••••••••••••••••••••••

John and Agnes were married for nearly thirty years. They raised several children but, regrettably, once the children were grown, John and Agnes were to be divorced. Like some couples, they stayed married much too long "for the sake of the children."

John was a staff sergeant in the military. He and his wife traveled about Europe, from military base to military base during John's career. Agnes occupied herself by doing bookkeeping, accounting, and tax work for American armed forces personnel. Agnes maintained the family books and records.

Over the years, Agnes had tolerated physical abuse and John's drinking. When she filed for divorce, Agnes packed up the family records and, having no children as baggage, returned to England to stay with her mother.

All of the couple's assets were liquid and kept in financial institutions. However, Agnes had been quite clever as the family accountant. She had maintained bank accounts in several financial institutions across Europe. Even though she and John were both United States citizens, she had left behind a cache of marital assets in each country where John had been assigned to a military base. After nearly three decades of marriage, they had little to show in their own names except for John's pension. John's drinking had gotten to the point where what little he might have known in the past became blurred.

Agnes consented to the divorce, and the parties split John's pension equally with a Qualified Domestic Relations Order (QDRO).

By the conclusion of the divorce, John was left with half his pension, the amount being modest. Agnes happily accepted the divorce decree from the mail carrier who delivered it to her in England, and John was left to wonder where, after all those years, their money had gone. Agnes didn't wonder, for the money was safely in Europe with her. Agnes generously had helped herself to ninety percent of the marital estate by being the responsible person in charge of the assets, cleverly concealing them, allowing her husband to stumble about in financial ignorance.

Moral of the Story
Know where the money is and how much is there. Keep full access to all family records. It may be costly and is sometimes impossible to recreate a trail of assets, particularly where one spouse has deliberately secreted assets and covered the trail by destroying records. If a marriage begins to deteriorate, keep an extra copy of all records safely, where your spouse cannot destroy them.

Going to the Cleaners

One of the most frequent threats heard in the context of divorce is the revengeful spouse who declares, "I am going to take you to the cleaners." When you hear that threat, you can be sure that somebody's worried about being cleaned and pressed! Yet, the threat of being *taken to the cleaners* is usually a toothless tiger rather than a reality.

The operating principle in divorce is a 50/50 split of the marital estate. One exception to this rule is where the burden of raising children is so great that the periodic payment of child support alone will not satisfy the needs of the children. Another exception to an equal division of the marital estate is your spouse being "at fault" for the breakdown of the marriage relationship.

Usually, child support is adequate to provide for the care,

maintenance, and other necessities of minor children. Most of the time, if the non-custodial parent is able and available for full time suitable work, child support alone can provide for the children's necessities.

If the non-custodial parent, however, is unemployed, under-employed, or unemployable, so that the amount of child support would be inadequate to take care of the children's needs, then the cus-todial parent might request a larger share of the assets than the normal 50/50 split.

Some courts alleviate the additional burden of raising children by allowing the custodial parent to occupy the marital home. This usually allows the custodial parent to reside there until the youngest child is age 18 or graduates from high school, the custodial parent remarries, or an unrelated person of the opposite sex moves in.

You might be "taken to the cleaners" when you have been at fault and your spouse can prove it. It is not enough that there has been some fault, the fault must be material and significant to the break-down of the marriage and the spouse who is accusing their partner of fault must generally be innocent, or comparatively less at fault.

Often, one spouse will accuse the other of marital infidelity. That is not a one-way street, however. The accused will often defend him/herself on the basis that their spouse drove them to being unfaith-ful by denying sexual relations during the marriage, by ostracizing them, by mental cruelty, or by some other negative force. Merely because your spouse has been "at fault" is no assurance that the mar-ital estate will be divided in any fashion other than 50/50.

Usually, the premium paid where one spouse was at fault is that they might only take 45% or 40% of the marital estate, instead of the usual one-half. Most courts are reluctant to divide the marital estate in any fashion other than equally. Even though one party might be guilty of fault over a protracted period, many courts are critical if the spouse who has been victimized didn't file for divorce.

A failure to file for divorce might constitute a waiver of your spouse's fault. If your spouse misbehaves, and you don't sue for divorce, you have tolerated this misbehavior. Few courts will reward you for having "sat on your hands" by not filing for divorce. There are few financial rewards for enduring marital martyrdom.

•••••••••••••••••••••••••••••••••

Chester and Jan had been married for nearly 30 years. They both held the same rank on a municipal police force. Each was close to retirement and had a pension that was substantially the same. However, Chester had fashioned himself the financial wizard of the marital relationship.

Over the years, Chester had taken many of the liquid assets of the marriage and invested them in a variety of tax shelters, all of which had fallen to the ground. He had purchased copper futures, tax shelters in library plates, and other bad investments which made Wall Street's junk bonds seem like an attractive investment. Chester was accused in the divorce proceedings of being "at fault" financially.

Jan brought evidence to the court showing that Chester had unilaterally and without her knowledge or consent helped himself to tens-of-thousands of dollars of marital assets whenever he saw fit, to invest in one bad deal or another.

Often, Chester would buy a piece of real estate as an investment, yet he would allow the tenants to move in without security deposits and would fail to evict them when they defaulted on the rent. On other occasions, he would swallow, hook, line, and sinker, the overly-generous misrepresentations of so-called "investment advisors" who sold him penny stocks which only diminished in value.

By demonstrating to the court that Chester's pattern and practice was one of unilateral action with marital assets invested in poor opportunities which repeatedly failed, Jan established that Chester was "at fault" financially.

The court did not award a 50/50 split but threatened to give a disproportionately larger share to Jan. This threat of an unequal division of the marital estate spurred the parties toward settlement of a 65% division of marital assets in favor of Jan.

Moral of the Story
Anticipate investment decisions. Know your return on investment, and which investments succeed or fail. If your spouse is involved in an pattern and practice of bad investments or deceit with regard to marital assets, either file for separate maintenance or divide the marital estate into separate accounts.

Those who continue to cohabit after there has been fault by the other spouse, whether financial irresponsibility or marital infidelity, may be deemed to have consented to the misbehavior. Those who suffer through marital martyrdom will not be rewarded by the divorce gods after years of tolerating a bad situation. Get out while the getting is good, or suffer the rebuke of an equal division of assets.

A Brand New Me

After Margie had been married to Elmer, but only for a few brief years, the divorce netted her practically nothing by way of a property settlement. Because of their short term marriage, the fact that they had no children, the fact that it was a second marriage for each, and the fact that they were both mature adults, each took from the marriage whatever they brought in and nothing more.

This infuriated Margie. Even though she had been married to Elmer but three years, she felt these were the *three best years of her life*, no doubt. Margie vowed revenge. Hell hath no fury like a lover scorned.

Margie's revenge was to remarry Elmer. Hardly had the divorce meats grown cold before they were reheated for the wedding feast. Margie's re-courtship of Elmer was a swift victory. Within months of the final divorce decree, Margie and Elmer had remarried each other.

Margie persuaded Elmer that he should enjoy the pleasures of her as a younger, remade woman. The Old Margie was about to be discarded and a new woman would emerge. Once remarried, Margie had the benefit of Elmer's dental coverage, hospital, medical, surgical, periodontal, podiatric, psychiatric, and all of the other of insurance which was guaranteed to release the New Margie.

Margie scheduled herself at the dentist and had all of her dentures reworked. She went to the podiatrist and had all of her corns and bunions fixed. She saw the opthamologist, and had new contact lenses prescribed and an extra set of glasses made. She scheduled a Day at the Spa *weekly*. Margie then persuaded Elmer that she would look much better with a face lift, a tummy tuck, and a little corrective surgery on that pronounced hook which some fashioned as a nose.

Of course, Elmer acceded to her every whim, wish, and desire. He acted partially out of guilt for his prior divorce and, somehow, Margie had persuaded Elmer that the Fountain of Youth could not be far behind once the New Margie emerged.

With the physical corrections, improvements, and remakes completed, Margie persuaded Elmer that she ought to have a new wardrobe. But how could he refuse? Having invested a small fortune in turning this Old Hen into a Spring Chicken, Elmer conceded. Margie bought one of everything for spring, summer, winter, and fall. Increasingly uncomfortable with the volume of dollars being invested in Margie's good looks and physical well being, Elmer began to murmur subtle protests. Margie was quick. At the sound of the first dissent, she would flail away at him with her whips of guilt. Elmer had begun to dig himself into a hole that he shared with Wilbur Milktoast.

As time passed, Elmer could only internalize his anger and stuff his feelings deeper and deeper. Elmer was an explosion waiting to happen. Indeed, in due time, the volcano of anger erupted, spewing forth a lava of divorce pleadings.

While the previous marriage to Margie had lasted a solid three years, the second one managed to drag itself out for twice as long. Not only had Margie become a new woman but, also, she had successfully wormed her way to becoming the co-owner and joint tenant on every asset that Elmer had previously owned by himself. Her name was added to the house because she threatened a temper tantrum at the closing when Elmer dredged up all of the cash from his individual retirement account (IRA) to purchase their new marital abode.

Margie insisted on being a joint tenant on every brokerage, bank, and financial account that Elmer owned. "Why, what would happen to me if something happened to you?" Margie would inquire.

By the time that Elmer began to scratch his "seven year itch," Margie had successfully and inextricably become intertwined in his very financial essence. She had not only created a *Brand New Me* but, also, had become a much wealthier woman in the process. Having nearly spent Elmer into the Poorhouse before he mustered the nerve to cry "Uncle," there was not a single asset left untouched when the divorce court examined the marital estate. Margie walked away from marriage #2 with the very bonanza that she had missed when divorce #1 was granted.

Moral of the Story
Be careful of marrying your *ex-* because there was some reason you got divorced in the first place; but, if you do, tread softly and carry a big prenuptial agreement. Otherwise, you will become

evidence of the ancient adage: hurt me once it's your fault; hurt me twice it's my fault.

Do You Really Want a Divorce?

Most people marry for love. Despite love, however, there are grounds for divorce. Grounds for divorce may include abandonment, desertion, voluntary separation, bigamy, felony conviction, impotence, mental cruelty, non-support and more. Nonetheless, you must ask: do you really want a divorce?

Divorce is a big decision. Divorce may be the most important decision you make in your adult life. Financially speaking, divorce is more profound than marriage.

Divorce is expensive. There will be attorney fees. In a contested divorce, with the normal range of difficult issues, each party may need to budget about 5% of your gross assets on attorney fees. There may be tax consequences when dividing up certain marital assets. If assets are sold, there can be sales commissions and the costs of sale.

Assets will be diminished. Your marital estate will be reduced substantially. In most situations, assets are divided equally. That means you will be only half as rich after divorce than when you were married.

Standard of living will be lower. With only half the assets, you borrowing power will be reduced. With or without less credit, you will enjoy a lower standard of living. Two live more cheaply than one.

Divorce is emotionally traumatic. Divorce is an emotional trauma for spouses, children if any, including the family pets. You will lose sleep, churn of much anger, and may become ill. It will take you as long to get over the divorce process as it took to go through the process itself.

Divorce is a legal free-for-all. Filing divorce is an act of war. It starts a legal battle which signals the end of love and starts a mutual assault aimed at who gets the most money in the end. Divorce is simply the dissolution of a legal partnership. It is never painless.

Your kids will hate you. Unless your children are victims of abuse, and your are the rescuer, your children will hate you for filing a divorce. There is still a stigma for children among their peers, though less so than in decades passed. The kids will be mad at both parents.

Divorce is a hassle. If you are involved in a divorce, you can set aside the first two years focusing on the battle. You will function at half-speed in the rest of your life. For the next two years after the divorce, you will spend the time recovering.

Getting the Divorce You Want

If you truly want a divorce, then you need to aim at some goals. List what you want from the divorce. Prioritize your needs. Attempt to attain them at minimum cost.

Get an agreed property settlement. The ideal divorce is the negotiated divorce. Bargain a property settlement. Figure our values and who gets what before you visit an attorney. If that cannot happen, then bargain your settlement before you go to trial. You really don't want a judge to try your case. Divorce trial are complex, boring, and nobody really wins.

Get a divorce that settles the issues. Your divorce should settle the issues. It should leave no unresolved questions. Problems should be resolved so that you don't have to return to court (for such issues as alimony, child custody, etc.).

Get the best deal possible. If you don't get a good deal now, you'll never be satisfied. Yes, you can walk away from a marriage.

Give everything to your spouse. Avoid the hassle. For some people, this works. Usually, you cannot afford to do so. In a divorce, you do what you have to do, whether it means cooperating fully or being less than candid about what's on your mind. If you get into a divorce, hang in there, do your scrapping, get the best deal possible, then put it behind you.

Divorce Planning Checklist

The decision to file for divorce cannot be an impulse decision. Indeed, where the stakes involve children or serious money, you must plan ahead. Consider implementing these protective devices *before filing the divorce complaint*:

CHECKLIST

- *If you're going to move anyway, then move.* If you intend to move after the divorce, and there are no children or joint-ly held real property, then liquidate your assets, take half and leave town. File for divorce after you move.

- *Incorporate your business.* If you own a business as a sole proprietorship or partnership, incorporate it. If this business will be yours after the divorce, it is relatively easy to place a low value on a new corporation.

- *Don't expand your business.* Divorces take concentration, effort, and time that you could be devoting to an enterprise. If you are in the throes of a divorce, your business will suffer. Wait until after the divorce to expand.

- *Change all beneficiaries.* After filing, you may not be allowed to change beneficiaries on wills, trusts, life insurance, annuities, certificates of deposit, individual retirement accounts (IRA), 401(k) plans, pensions, and the like. Discreetly make desired changes before filing.

- *Cash in all unnecessary insurance.* Divorce courts frequently issue *status quo* orders, continuing insurance plans in effect during the divorce. Consider cancelling insurance in for cash value and living off the proceeds; stop insurance property not titled in your name.

- *Confiscate, cancel and cut-up all credit cards.* Any credit card for which you are liable, as cardholder or guarantor, must be cancelled in writing, certified mail, return receipt requested. If you don't you will wish you did.

- *Secure all financial and family records.* Empty the safety deposit box. Make copies or take possession of all tax returns, mortgage and loan applications, financial statements, credit card statements, deeds to property, insurance records, bank statements, mortgage records, and other valuables.

- *Secure all liquid assets.* Close out all joint bank accounts and place all liquid assets in your own name. Checking accounts, savings accounts, cash-on-hand, stocks, savings bonds, certificates of deposit, safety deposit boxes, coins, jewelry, and other valuable collections. Leave no liquid asset accessible to your spouse.

- *Defer promotions or raises.* Swap perquisites for cash until the divorce is done. Income determines child support and alimony. In fact, if you could, you might offer a salary decrease in exchange for a company car.

- *Get a job — for your spouse.* If your spouse is unemployed or underemployed, that means you will be the one providing support. The more self-sufficient your spouse is, the less you pay. Urge your spouse to finish their education, get recertified, or take vocational training.

- *Quit your job.* If you've always wanted to go to graduate school, be a writer, or switch to a more satisfying (but lower paying) job, quit the rat race now. If you wait until after the judge sets the amount for child or spousal support, you'll never be able to afford taking the plunge.

- *Start kids' on special programs.* Before filing, start treatment with the psychologist, begin the four-year program at the orthodontist, or enroll a child in private school. Courts will often order a continuation of the *status quo*, but will rarely order new programs to begin.

- *Accelerate major credit purchases.* Married couples are more creditworthy than recent divorcees. Before filing, remortgage the house and purchase the new car while you still enjoy joint credit.

- *Transfer titles to joint property.* Parents will often keep children as joint on bank accounts, real property, or other assets. These can be seen for marital assets and allocated by the divorce judge, particularly where that parent dies during your divorce.

- *Past the 20 year mark.* The Social Security Administration allows one spouse (married for 20 years, but who has not worked outside the house) to keep their working spouse's social security after that working spouse dies. Get beyond the 20 year mark if you're close.

- *Bury a nest egg.* Stash away some cash, whether in the name of a trusted friend or in a foreign account. You may need emergency money to move out or pay your lawyer. Keep a reserve fund for the rainy day — storm's coming!

Grounds for Divorce

Do you have grounds for divorce? In most places, it doesn't matter what your grounds are for divorce. These jurisdictions operate under the law of "no fault" divorce. Nobody has to be at fault if the marriage is broken down and there is no chance of preserving it. The language differs from place to place: some statutes require an "irretrievable breakdown of the marriage" with "no reasonably likelihood that the marriage can be preserved."

Where some degree of fault is required, some laws itemize the type of fault which must exist, while other statutes merely give examples of the kinds of fault which entitled a married person to a divorce. These are among the litany of faults which many states recognize:

- *Abandonment*, separation, desertion, refusal to cohabitate with spouse).

- *Abuse* of spouse or children.

- *Adultery*.

- *Addiction* to drugs, alcohol, gambling, etc.

- *Bigamy* (already married).

- *Crime* (felony conviction or infamous crime, attempted murder of spouse).

- *Cruelty* (physical, mental)

- *Disease* (infecting spouse with venereal disease; Hansen's disease; impotency; insanity).

- *Duress* or force in marrying.

- *Incapacity* to consent to marriage.
- *Incompatibility*, intolerable severity, perversion, wickedness.

- *Non-support.*

- *Pregnancy* at marriage.

Some places require that a the basis for the fault will have continued for a minimum period. For example, if the basis is a felony conviction, often the spouse must have actually served one to three years of the sentence.

Divorce Questionnaire

If you are not dissuaded yet from considering divorce, then take the test. Indicate which of the following statements is true.

QUESTIONNAIRE

I WANT A DIVORCE BECAUSE ...   TRUE?

My marriage is totally destroyed.   _____
There's no reason to stay married.   _____
There's no chance to save my marriage.   _____
My spouse and I are incompatible.   _____
Communications are broken down.   _____
My spouse physically abuses me.   _____
My spouse emotionally abuses me.   _____
My spouse verbally abuses me.   _____
My spouse is an alcoholic.   _____
My spouse is a druggie.   _____
My spouse is a gambling addict.   _____
My spouse is addicted to shopping.   _____
My spouse is unfaithful.   _____
My spouse wastes our money.   _____
My spouse won't get a good job.   _____
My spouse won't let me get the job I want.   _____
Our child rearing ideas conflict.   _____
Our ideas of family size conflict.   _____
I can pursue a relationship with _____.   _____
My spouse is too fat.   _____
My spouse has bad personal hygiene.   _____

A DIVORCE WOULDN'T BOTHER ME IF I ...
Had to move from where I live.   _____
Lost custody of my child(ren).   _____
Had to deal with alimony.   _____
Had to deal with child support.   _____
Had less money than before.   _____
Got no social security.   _____

TOTAL...   _____

Now that you have taken the test, count the number of true answers and study your options.

SCORE CARD

TRUE	OPTIONS
None	Smile
1 - 5	Start Talking
6 - 22	Visit a Marriage Counselor
23 - 27	Hire a Divorce Lawyer

If all statements are false ... then count your blessings, keep smiling and, after you have read this book, pass it along to a friend in need.

chapter 3 THE DIVORCE ATTORNEY

One Attorney is *Nobody's Lawyer*

Some optimistic parties to a divorce think they can hire one lawyer and save fees. In theory, it is possible to hire one lawyer. An attorney can ethically represent both parties, under such circumstances where each party understands the consequences of having one lawyer, and consents to the arrangement.

This type of one-lawyer divorce is only practicable where the parties have mutually agreed to all material aspects of the divorce; the attorney's role then is to prepare the necessary paperwork to reflect the agreement of the parties. In most cases, however, one-lawyer divorces are ill-advised and, threaten to be unethical.

In some instances, parties perceive that they agree on all material matters but, in reality, this is not so. What happens when a material issue arises which neither party contemplated but which must be resolved? The attorney knows how a resolution of a disputed issue can help one client, but be adverse to the other. This places the attorney in an ethical dilemma which can be resolved in only one way— someone has to hire their own lawyer.

If you and your spouse are of one mind to hire the same lawyer, and you visit an attorney for a consultation, the good lawyer will represent only one party. It's acceptable to have only one lawyer involved as long as it is clear who is the client. There should be a clear understanding as to who is represented by that attorney. It must be made perfectly clear that if an issue arises where the parties have adverse positions and cannot mutually agree on how to resolve that conflict, the attorney must represent the plaintiff; at that point, the attorney must also advise both clients that they each must have their own separate counsel.

Do not involve yourself in a situation where there is one lawyer representing both parties unless you get a clear understanding, from the beginning, that if any dispute arises—the attorney will represent you, not your spouse. No doubt, one attorney is nobody's lawyer.

Hiring a Specialist

The best matrimonial attorneys consider themselves divorce specialists. Just because someone has graduated from law school, passed the bar exam, and holds a license to practice law does not automatically qualify them to practice divorce law.

If your divorce is simple, there is no real property, no personal property of any consequence, and no issues regarding children (support, visitation, or custody) or alimony, then almost any attorney should be able to get you divorced. For a simple divorce, a specialist is not required and you should not pay a generous retainer to accomplish the task. As matters become increasingly complex, however, you need greater legal expertise.

The lawyer's attitude is the key to your selection. You must be able to deal with that attorney easily and effectively. Working together, as a team, is critical.

A divorce specialist will be an excellent negotiator, with specialized knowledge in the family law arena. The specialist will be charming, with a good sense of humor, and a reasoned thinker. Never intentionally offensive. Generally speaking, a nice person. Down deep, however, the divorce specialist will slit your throat and enjoy the process.

The specialist is not your psychologist and does very little "hand-holding." Matrimonial specialists don't run divorce mills. Principally, they play high stakes poker with your money and win for you, where you are too emotionally wrecked to think straight.

Substantial assets require not only a divorce specialist, but one who has a strong accountancy background. Issues of assets and liabilities in divorce may seem simple, but can become complex. Issues of valuation are often hotly contested.

Values of a closely-held corporation (such as a family business) can range tremendously, depending upon many variables. With this type of asset, particularly when the closely-held business accrued value while the parties were married, a divorce specialist is appropriate—particularly one with a strong business background.

Complex issues involving children require a divorce specialist. For example, the issue of child custody may seem simple enough but, if contested, it requires a matrimonial practitioner to effectively present the best argument. Similarly, issues of child support, and child visitation, will require particular expertise in family law.

A marriage which presents an alimony issue particularly when one spouse has nurtured a career while the other has not worked outside of the household, can require the services of a divorce specialist. Alimony has serious, long-term cash flow impact as well as federal and state tax implications. Here,be sure that your divorce specialist also has a keen grasp of income tax issues or employs an accountant who does.

Special assets, which the inexperienced attorney may not recognize as marital assets, require a specialist. For example, pension plans, annuities, individual retirement accounts (IRA's), 401(k) plans, and the like, all present serious issues of valuation and allocation. Some special assets are unique, such as the value of a professional degree (earned by one spouse during the marriage at the expense of substantial marital dollars). Other special assets may include accrued leave time (vacation pay, sick leave, personal days) which can be converted to a cash value upon termination from employment. These special assets might not be recognized as marital assets to be divided during a divorce by a general practitioner.

Litigation expertise is needed if your divorce goes to trial. This expertise, even among experienced divorce practitioners, is uncommon. Very few divorces ever go to trial. Perhaps only one percent of all the divorces actually go to a full-fledged trial and are resolved by a judge or referee after a complete evidentiary hearing. However, when a trial does occur, it is not only important to be represented by a divorce law specialist, but also by someone who has an excellent track record as a civil litigator in the matrimonial arena.

Expert Witnesses

The divorce issues most often litigated include alimony, child custody, and the division of assets. Where there are complicated issues, expert witnesses may be required to help the judge appreciate facts which may not be obvious to the court:

Child custody issues might require expert testimony; psychiatrists, psychologists, social workers, and teachers might testify about which custodial environment is in the best interests of the child.

Pension and annuity problems require actuaries to testify as to the present value of pensions or a future income stream from a pension plan.

Alimony disputes can benefit from testimony of vocational retraining experts concerning the employability of a spouse who has principally devoted their marital time to raising children and maintaining a household.

Business valuation disagreements can be determined with the help of a certified public accountant to testify on the value of a business which is closely held and family operated.

Real property values can be set forth by real estate appraisers and real estate brokers to testify as to true cash value.

Expert testimony can be used on many divorce issues. An experienced trial practitioner will to make the best use of experts on your behalf and can effectively cross-examine experts called by your spouse.[1] If your divorce is one of those rare cases which goes to trial, you may consider asking your attorney, if not a seasoned trial practitioner, to refer your case to an experienced litigator who can best handle that complex stage of the proceedings.

Divorce Appeals

If your divorce has gone to trial and an adverse judgment has been entered, your case may be one of those rare divorces which goes to an appeal. Very few divorces ever go to an appellate court. Matters which do go up on appeal require an expert appellate attorney, capable of handling the difficult task of drafting an appeal brief and arguing orally before a panel of appellate judges.

If your case is appealed, be sure your lawyer has the special expertise and track record necessary to effectively represent you at the appellate level. It is wise to retain an appellate specialist to handle the brief-writing and oral argument of a complex, bitterly-contested, or high asset divorce. The appellate stage of divorce proceedings requires particular expertise; do not hesitate to seek special counsel.

---

1 See *The Trial Practice Guide* by Joan M. Brovins and Thomas Oehmke (1992 American Bar Ass'n, Chicago, Illinois).

Panning for Gold — or a Lawyer

Getting a good divorce lawyer, and one who will suit your personality and case, is a difficult undertaking. Nearly every lawyer practices divorce, but few lawyers practice it well. With a simple divorce, involving no issues as to children, property, or alimony, your search for a divorce lawyer should probably begin by letting your "fingers do the walking" through the Yellow Pages. If your divorce harbors potentially complex issues, then your search must be more serious than that of the ordinary consumer of legal services.

A referral from a satisfied client is one lead to a divorce attorney. Of course, you would need to know something about the type of case that this satisfied client had, as well as the competency of the attorney involved. But how do you discover something about competency?

After obtaining a referral, look in the Yellow Pages for some indication of the type of ad, if any, the suggested attorney has placed. Of course, Yellow Pages advertising is purchased and an attorney can say anything in such ads; however, if the referred attorney happens to have a Yellow Pages ad indicates a concentration, specialty, or interest in divorce, that is a favorable indicator.

You could check out the referral attorney with the bar association in the county where your divorce will be filed. Because each judge handles divorce issues slightly differently, it is important that your attorney can offer some prediction as to how a given judge will rule on a particular issue. That type of local practice expertise is unique. You might also ask the local Bar Association to categorize attorneys by their areas of expertise. However, if an attorney expresses an interest in obtaining family law referrals, this is an additional, favorable indicator. You might learn if the referral attorney is among the lawyers suggested by the local bar association for divorce matters.

Ask if the referral attorney (or whose advertising you have

been attracted to) is an active participant in the family law or divorce section of the local bar association. Of course, participation alone is no guarantee of expertise; however, subject matter interest is a trait consistent with expertise. Standing alone, none of these criteria will indicate whether one is a good divorce attorney; nonetheless, all of these indicators are important in your overall assessment of a potential legal advocate for your case.

Another approach which some find successful is to interview several attorneys. This gives you some indication as to whether your personality meshes with a prospective lawyer. The ability to place trust in an advocate and feel confident in the advice given are critical. Also, you can learn something about an attorney merely by the way they keep their office, how their staff interacts with you, and their approach to your interview. Be prepared, however, to pay for the privilege. When you call an attorney to schedule an interview, be clear that you are seeking a divorce advocate and offer to pay their hourly fee customarily associated with such an interview.

Be wary of getting the first interview free; you usually get what you pay for and deserve what you get — nothing! If an attorney is giving away time, free of charge for the first interview, the attorney either does not have enough work to keep busy or is not necessarily going to give you the "time of day." If your interview is rushed and if you do not have the opportunity to articulate the issues which concern you, then you will not be the wiser for having traveled this path.

Another benefit to interviewing an attorney and paying for the time you employ is to get some perspective as to how a local judge might handle the one or two critical issues in your divorce. After interviewing several attorneys, you should begin to hear the same range of responses (though not exactly the same answer in each case). This approach indicates whether the attorney whom you ultimately select is generally on track in addressing you particular problem.

In conducting your interview, it is not only important to hear what the attorney says, but to assess how it is said to you. Even more important than the answers you receive are the list of questions which the attorney will ask you. Thorough attorneys will solicit a substantial amount of information from you before even beginning to address what, to you, may seem to be the most simple questions. Be prepared to answer those questions asked. Consider the nature of the questions asked as important indicators of the type of attorney with whom you are dealing.

Ask certain pointed questions of each attorney with whom you speak, including: the estimated range of fees and hourly rate which would be charged in your case; the length of time it may take to process your divorce; the types of issues which the attorney can readily identify might be problematic; the types of experts, if any, which the attorney would utilize and the associated expenses; and the difficulties which the attorney sees will have to be confronted and resolved in your case before a final judgment of divorce would be entered.

You should feel free to ask of your prospective attorney these types of questions:

QUESTIONS

Personal   What do you like about divorce practice? Ever been divorced? How will your religion affect the advice you may give me? Ever been disciplined by the bar association or attorney grievance commission? Ever been sued for malpractice?

Education   What classes or seminars have you taken or taught in area of divorce, litigation, or appeals?

Law Practice   Years practicing law? Percent of husbands versus wives you represent? How may divorces have you handled from complaint to judgment?   What percent of your practice is divorce? Who are your support staff?

Credentials   Member of the local bar association's family law committee? Any honorary memberships (such as the American Academy of Matrimonial Lawyers)?

Issues   What are the important issues in my case? What's the likely outcome of these contested issues in your divorce?

Experts   Who is the accountant, tax or financial analyst you suggest we use, if any?

Judges   Who are the judges favorable or unfavorable to the issues in my case (child support, custody, alimony, or tax)?

Local County   What percent of your divorces go to trial? Are appealed? What are the results?

Opponent   What is the reputation of my spouse's attorney?   Who are the other good divorce lawyers in town that my spouse might retain?

Trials   What types of civil or criminal cases have you taken to judge trial? Jury trial? How many divorce cases have you ever taken to trial during the last five years? What were the contested issues (custody, visitation, support, property distribution)?

Appeals   How many divorce cases have you taken to the appellate court level?

<u>*Publications*</u>   What articles or books have you written on legal subjects, including divorce?

<u>*Fees & Costs*</u>   What is your hourly rate for my divorce? The retainer? What costs will you bill me for and at what rate? Will I get a monthly, itemized bill, showing who did what, how long it took, and how much it cost?

Some attorneys may find such questions impertinent. However, as a potential client and one who may spend thousands of dollars with that attorney, you are certainly entitled to ask these questions.

A confident practitioner would be willing to give you an honest response, especially if you're paying for the interview. The information you receive should be assimilated before you make your ultimate choice of counsel. Some negative answers to these questions do not necessarily mean that attorney cannot do an excellent job representing you. However, hear all of the answers and to make your decision based on the totality of the circumstances.

It is also interesting to ask prospective attorneys what they think of the other attorneys whom you have interviewed. You should not be shy about admitting that you have talked to, or intend to speak with, other prospective counsel. A good attorney should not necessarily bad-mouth or negatively rate every other practitioner. Be wary of the attorney who trashes all the other lawyers in town and stands on a pedestal purporting to be the only person who can handle your case under these circumstances.

The Price is Right

It costs a little money to be married, but it costs real money to be divorced. The process is normally too complex for the lay person to act without counsel. This is not an unreasonable expectation when you consider the financial consequences of what transpires in a divorce proceeding.

More money changes hands in divorce litigation than in all other civil litigation combined. Most trial court dockets are divided into roughly three equal parts: criminal, civil, and divorce. The typical divorce, however, involves dividing a marital estate that is valued at $100,000 or more on the average. The value of the typical marital estate far exceeds the average settlement paid in a civil litigation case.

Considering the economics of divorce, it is imperative that one acquire the services of a good attorney who is well-versed in this type of law. But what price to pay?

Examination of the classified ads or the yellow pages reveal a variety of attorneys supposedly willing to secure your divorce for mere dollars. Some parties can benefit from less expensive legal services such as these.

Marriages where there is no real property, no substantial assets, no children, and no alimony issues can benefit from low cost, basic legal services which you find advertised in the classifieds and yellow pages. However, a divorce where there are substantial assets, or a valuable home, or issues of child custody, support, visitation, or alimony deserve the best legal care you can afford.

Where the parties agree on how to resolve all issues and seek the services of a lawyer to merely "prepare the papers," you might expect to pay between $250 or so (plus or minus actual court costs). However, even where simple issues are in dispute (even if only the amount of child support to be paid), you might expect to pay $750 or so, assuming no major battles ensue.

Nonetheless, where matters become more complex, where there are issues of spouse abuse, assets where substantial values are disputed, contests as to child custody, or the amount of income that should be considered for child support, quality legal services are required. You might typically expect to pay $1,500 to $4,500 or more, depending on the amount of disagreement and how long the contested battle drags on.

Where marriage has spanned several decades and the accumulation of a wide variety of assets has occurred, often the financial battle is furious. Warfare is waged. In such circumstances, it is not uncommon to spend from $7,500 to $15,000 on a divorce. However, it is important to keep in mind that missing one asset, or under-valuing a significant asset, can cost that much alone by a single mistake.

•••••••••••••••••••••••••••••••

Ernie and Marilyn were married for nearly 25 years. Ernie worked as a psychologist at a state institution. As was customary with government service, the public sector was very generous with sick days, vacation days, personal leave days, personal business days, and more. Ernie's employer had a policy of allowing employees to "bank" unused leave time. Over the course of his long-term employment, Ernie had accumulated more than 2,000 hours of paid leave time. Upon his retirement, Ernie was eligible to receive this leave time paid in a lump sum.

During the course of the marriage, if Ernie had used this leave time, Ernie would have spent more time with his family. The accumulated value of this employment benefit was a cash asset upon retirement. As his "retirement gift" to himself, Ernie filed for divorce. His wife, remembering that Ernie had accumulated substantial leave time, claimed the accumulated cash value of the leave time as a "marital asset." It had accrued during the marriage and should benefit both spouses.

The court agreed and Ernie's lump sum payment — which was the equivalent of one year's pay — was equally divided as a marital asset because that asset had accrued during the marriage. As Ernie's salary was $45,000 per year upon retirement, that asset alone was worth $22,500 to Ernie's soon-to-be ex-wife.

Moral of the Story
You get what you pay for, and that includes divorce attorneys. Be

careful of the divorce done "on the cheap." You may save money now but it could cost you later. The divorce path is strewn with subtleties that can only be identified and properly valued with time and care. The money you pay to a divorce attorney is an investment in preserving your fair share of the assets.

The Other Lawyer

Your spouse's attorney — the opposing counsel — is a "hired gun," just as your lawyer is!

Many divorce litigants focus their anger on the opposing attorney, often wondering aloud how that lawyer can do *such a thing*. Remember, the role of your spouse's attorney is to advocate and do the best job possible for your spouse, not you. Lawyers are retained as advocates. They do battle like gladiators in place of the actual disputants.

Nonetheless, there is a medicinal benefit to focus your anger on the opposing attorney. That adversary deflects anger that might otherwise be focused at your spouse during the course of this troubling litigation. Making your spouse angry only makes matters worse.

Will the opposing attorney try to lie, cheat, and steal? Possibly. Will the opposing attorney threaten to "take you to the cleaners"? There is a chance. Will the opposing attorney consume the marital estate in attorney fees (which you are expected to pay)? That, too, cannot be ruled out.

All of these factors must be kept in mind as you develop a respect for your opponent, not unlike the respect that everyone ought to have for a loaded .38 caliber revolver or an 18-wheeler rolling down the expressway at 75 miles per hour. Fear is a good thing, particularly when it generates healthy respect.

What a Wimp

Sometimes the opposing attorney is a less than challenging adversary. When your opponent has gas where there should be guts, be quiet and be grateful. In other words, if your spouse's attorney is an ineffective advocate, perhaps not so bright in the area of accounting, or inarticulate in the courtroom, or stumbling during negotiations, learn to keep your mouth shut.

To often during divorce litigation, spouses speak with each other about their respective counsel. It is not uncommon to hear one party chiding their partner about the opposing "stupid lawyer" or about what a "dumb thing" their adversary did. This is foolish talk that gains nothing and causes your spouse to think that they should switch attorneys.

If the opposing attorney for your spouse is about as effective as a lump on a log then, to slur a metaphor, let sleeping logs lie.

My Lawyer Can Beat Your Lawyer

If you are fortunate enough to have hired the most stellar gladiator to advocate for you in divorce proceedings, then do not parade around in public pronouncing your profound admiration for the unmatched skills of your attorney. Skilled negotiators and the most effective attorneys are not braggarts and tend to substitute substance for style. That is, an effective divorce attorney is often low keyed, extremely intelligent, articulate, and well-versed in economics and accounting.

The effective advocate will quietly proceed to gather together the facts necessary to earn you a fair split of the assets and avoid adverse economic and personal consequences. The attorney who struts around with feathers protruded like a peacock on parade is not an asset, but a danger.

If your lawyer can beat the other lawyer, then accept that fact with quiet confidence.

The fact that your lawyer may be more skilled and a better adversary is rewarded with results. If you obtain what you wish and if you pay a fair amount, that is what counts. You will pay dearly for good legal counsel, but advertising that fact to your spouse only exposes your achilles heel.

Researching the Opponent

Most divorce litigants have a morbid curiosity about the qualities and characteristics of the opposing counsel. Some pursue this curiosity by asking their attorney questions about the opposing counsel: What law school? How big is the firm? Do they really know what they're doing? How much to *they* charge?

Your attorney should be able to give you some insight as to the qualities and characteristics of opposing counsel. But if you are really curious, attorneys and firms may tout their accomplishments in a national publication called the *Martindale Hubbell Law Directory*. Ask your attorney to provide you with the opponent's listing information in that publication. Also, West Publishing Company carries an on-line database detailing the qualifications of many attorneys across the country and this may provide some insight.

For the most part, it is difficult to "research" the opposing counsel. The best clues as to the qualifications and characteristics of your opponent come from reviewing their written material (particularly motions and briefs that are filed in your case with the court) combined with observing their oral argument in the courtroom (with regard to motions before the friend of the court or the judge), and assessing their demeanor in the course of settlement negotiations.

Moral of the Story

If your lawyer is a "hot shot", then treat that information like a state secret: keep it to yourself. If the opposing attorney is incompetent, don't mention the fact, just enjoy it. Don't waste substantial effort researching the opposing counsel; the proof is in the pudding. Actions speak louder than words.

Attorney Fees at Twice the Price

Each spouse can petition the court to order that their attorney fees be paid by the other spouse. Most states provide that either spouse can be awarded some or all of their attorney fees; however, a few states still only allow a wife to seek attorney fees. Some attorney fees are awarded due to indigence and as sanctions against a party who takes a frivolous position on a contested issue.

Indigence would mean that, without an attorney fee award, the poorer spouse would not have enough money to hire and attorney and prosecute or defend the divorce. Some court routinely order the employed spouse to pay from $350 to $750 toward attorney fees on behalf of an unemployed spouse. However, if there is adequate property divided between the parties, then each is expected to pay their own attorney fees from the proceeds of their property settlement.

Sanctions against an unreasonable spouse can take the form of an attorney fee award. Some judges refer divorces to mediators who try to broker a voluntary settlement between the parties. If both parties accept the proposed settlement, then the case is settled and a judgment enters. However, if one party refused the voluntary settlement, the case goes to trial.

If the verdict of the court is consistent with the relief requested by the party who accepted the mediation award, then the court may order the unreasonable, rejecting party to pay attorney fees for both parties. This use of attorney fees (to sanction an unreasonable party) minimizes leveraging by the wealthier party.

chapter 4 SPOUSE ABUSE

Spouse Abuse Injunctions

Spouse abuse used to be one of those dirty family secrets about which no one spoke. Like so many types of abuses over the last several years, spouse abuse has "come out of the closet" and into the daylight.

Divorce judges are empowered to issue orders governing the behavior of the parties involved in divorce litigation. An injunction can be issued to prevent the misbehavior of one spouse against another during divorce proceedings and even after a final judgment is entered. If a divorce court enjoins one spouse from harassing, harming, assaulting, beating, or mocking the other, this is referred to as a spouse abuse injunction. Such injunctions may carry civil or criminal sanctions.

Civil spouse injunctions can be obtained when one spouse threatens to abuse another or where there is a legitimate apprehension (based on past behavior or other actions) which lead a spouse to fear for their own safety or the safety of their children. Normally, spouse abuse injunctions apply to married couples. Such injunctions may prohibit one or both spouses from entering onto the premises of the other spouse. These spouse abuse injunctions are served both on the spouse whose behavior is to be restricted as well as on the local police agency where both parties reside or work.

Spouse abuse injunctions are available for the protection of the parties in actions to annul a marriage, for a divorce, or separate maintenance. The court can act *ex parte* (without notifying the offending spouse before the court acts). Such injunction relief prohibits the opposing party from restraining their spouse's personal liberty during the pendency of the divorce.

A temporary restraining order, if issued *ex parte*, allows the spouse (whose behavior has been restricted) to come to court, upon short notice, and argue why that injunction should be set aside. A preliminary injunctive order can be issued to restrain a spouse from:

- Entering onto the premises; and,

- Assaulting, beating, molesting, or wounding their spouse; and,

- Removing minor children from the parent who has been given, by the court's order, legal custody of those children.

After a preliminary injunction is issued, the clerk of the court usually files a certified copy of that order with local law enforcement agencies who have jurisdiction over the place where each party resides.

A criminal spouse injunction is an order of the court which, if violated, usually allows a local police agency to arrest the offending spouse without first having to obtain an arrest warrant. On its face, a spouse abuse injunction will state whether or not it carries criminal sanctions. There is a notice to the offending spouse that if they refuse to comply with that order, they will be subject to the contempt powers of the court; if found guilty, such offending spouse can be imprisoned and/or fined in most circumstances.

In the past, some judges have routinely entered what is called a "mutual spouse abuse injunction with criminal sanctions." Some judges have been too eager to grant a criminal spouse injunction and, not wanting to put one spouse at risk, the courts would tend to criminally enjoin both spouses from misbehavior. On its face, this seems to be harmless. If one spouse behaves and the other spouse is a deviant, then the one who is well-behaved should — under most circumstances — have nothing to fear. But, that is not always the case.

You're Going to Jail

James and Sally were married for almost fifteen years. During the marriage, they raised some children. However, things changed with Sally after they were married. She had suffered mental illness and emotional disturbances which made her irrational and hysterical sometimes and often unreasonable.

Sally could not tolerate that James had filed for divorce. She needed the support of all of her friends and relatives ... from around the country. Sally did not hesitate to telephone long distance all of the time, day or night. Within a month of the divorce having been filed, the telephone bill had soared from practically nothing to hundreds of dollars.

James and Sally talked, but she refused to change her telephone habits while divorce was pending. Consequently, James removed the telephones from the house because he could not afford the telephone bills. Immediately, after James removed the phones, Sally rushed to the corner party store, clutching coins in hand, and telephoned the local police.

Sally indicated to the dispatcher that her husband had "ripped the phones from the walls," throwing them at her. In fact, when the police responded to Sally's hysteria, they did find the phones missing from the walls, but there was no evidence that the phones were thrown about. Indeed, if a phone had been thrown, it had left no mark nor had any phone instrument actually struck Sally. The police dutifully made a report and left.

In retaliation for her husband having removed the telephones, Sally went "on strike." She refused to shop, refused to prepare any meals, and let the food in the refrigerator go to waste. In fact, the contents of the refrigerator had become a proverbial "science experiment." Frustrated that her tactics were not working, Sally grabbed for more change and hustled to the corner store. This time, she called the police to report that her husband was trying to poison her. The police, again, quickly responded, only to find that Sally's version of "poisoning" meant that the family refrigerator had a spoiled stock pile of inedible foodstuffs. Again, the police dutifully made their report and left the "crime scene."

The police department had kept a file on this particular household because the court had issued a mutual spouse abuse injunction with criminal sanctions. However, nothing of what Sally had reported to the police was strictly prohibited by the injunctive order.

Over the coming weeks, Sally's telephone complaints to the police, all of which brought prompt response, included the following: James swore at me and said the "*F*—-" word; James came home late at night, drunk, and woke the household, "disturbing the peace"; James grabbed me by the wrists and hurt me (but only after Sally had admittedly tried to slam James upside the head with her frying pan). Imagine the exasperation of the police in responding to Sally's cries of abuse — but, the whole affair was about to culminate.

One warm Friday evening, before the sun had set, James was outside raking the lawn. Sally had stomped outside, in her bare feet, insisting that James come inside immediately to help her with some chore. These two had been living together for many months after their divorce was filed and the tension in the household had become intolerable.

Sally insisted. James refused. Sally insisted, again. James continued stubbornly to rake the lawn. Sally put her foot down, this time ... right in the pathway of James' rake.

There was a scream that could be heard in Timbuktu. Sally cried "bloody murder." She looked down at her foot and, unremarkably, the rake had scratched her baby toe and, if you looked carefully enough, you could almost see the faint beginnings of a drop of blood. Bare footed, screaming at the top of her lungs, Sally grabbed more coins and dashed to the telephone located on the corner to, once more, summon the *gendarmes*.

Sally screamed into the telephone, "he *raked* me, he *raked* me, and he's going to *rake* me again." The dispatcher from the police department calmed her down only long enough to record her infamous address. Tearing the phone out of the wall is one thing, but *rake* is a whole different matter. Lights and sirens, squad cars to the rescue, the police arrived in force, billy clubs in hand.

When the squad cars arrived at the home of Sally and James, Sally sat sobbing on the front porch, weeping relentlessly, breathlessly muttering something about being raped or raked or whatever it was. The police could hardly decipher her complaint amidst her sobs.

"You see, you see," she pointed to her scarlet toe, as her sobs toned down to a whimper. "He took that rake and dragged it across my toe deliberately. You see, he raked me!"

The police officers rolled their eyes up to the roof of their brains, and back down again. They took one look at Sally and another harder look at James standing there like the American Gothic, holding the lawn rake.

"Buddy," the police officer said to James, "we're sick and tired of *your wife* complaining. *You're* going to jail!"

Decisively, the two police officers grabbed James, handcuffed him, and put him in the police car, leaving Sally and the rake behind.

James spent the rest of Friday night and Saturday, as well as a good portion of Sunday in jail. The sheriff refused to release him, citing the criminal spouse abuse injunction as the authority for arresting James and holding him until arraignment.

On Sunday morning, a magistrate issued a writ of *habeas corpus* (an order compelling the prisoner to be removed from jail and brought before the court). The sheriff refused to honor the writ of *habeas corpus*, citing that a magistrate had no authority to issue such an extraordinary writ.

When all else had failed in that tough union town, James sought the assistance of the president of a UAW Local. What the magistrate could not do with the extraordinary writ of *habeas corpus*, the union president quickly accomplished. With one telephone call from the Local president to the sheriff, James was released from jail. He didn't go home that evening, but instead found himself a room at the local hotel, fearful of being charged again with the rake of his wife.

When the court held its hearing the following week on Sally's allegations of criminal spouse abuse, the judge dismissed the charges and dissolved the criminal spouse abuse injunction against James, but keeping it in effect against Sally.

Moral of the Story
Be careful of mutual criminal spouse abuse injunctions. They should beissued only against spouses who have actually threatened to assault, beat, molest, or wound the other. However, with police report, physicians statements, and hospital records in hand, don't hesitate to seek a spouse abuse injunction where the situation commands. Finally, be careful when raking the lawn, particularly when somebody puts their foot down.

Sample Spouse Abuse Injunction
Although the format may vary from state to state, the follow-

ing is a sample spouse injunction for the State of Michigan (with criminal sanctions). **State of Michigan**
[County] County Circuit Court

[Plaintiff],   Case No. [Number]
       Plaintiff
vs.   Hon. [Judge]
       Circuit Judge
[Defendant],
       Defendant

[Attorney]
Attorney for Plaintiff
[Street Address]
[City], [State] [Zip]
[Phone]

[Attorney]
Attorney for Defendant
[Street Address]
[City], [State] [Zip]
[Phone]

Ex Parte Mutual
Spouse Abuse Injunction
[with Criminal Sanctions]

At a session of said Court
held in the chambers of
the above-referenced Judge on

PRESENT: Hon. [Judge]
Circuit Judge

Upon reading the verified Motion of *[Plaintiff]* and it appearing that immediate and irreparable injury and damage will result to *[Plaintiff]* unless an Ex Parte Injunctive Order is issued without notice to *[Defendant]* and the Court being fully advised in the premises; it is hereby. . .

ORDERED that both *[Plaintiff]* and *[Defendant]* (as well as any officers, agents, servants, employees, attorneys and those persons in active concert or participation with either party who receives actual notice of this Order by personal service or otherwise) DO ABSOLUTELY DESIST AND REFRAIN FROM:

A. Assaulting, beating, wounding, or molesting the other party, or

B. Entering onto the other party's premises, namely *[Defendant]* may not enter *[Plaintiff's]* home at *[Plaintiff's Address]* and *[Plaintiff]* may not enter *[Defendant's]* home at *[Defendant's Address]*.

C. Removing any of the following minor children from *[Custodial Parent]* (who is the spouse having legal custody of such child[ren]) in violation of a custody and visitation order, as previously issued by the Court, the child[ren] being *[Child] [Date of Birth]*, now age *[age]*; and, it is further. . .

ORDERED that this Injunction shall be valid upon personal service on *[Plaintiff]* and *[Defendant]* and shall continue for one year from date of entry unless extended by further Order of this Court; and, it is further. . .

ORDERED that failure to comply with the terms of this injunction will subject you to criminal contempt of court as provided in section 15(a), Chapter 4, section 4(a), Chapter 9, and section 14(a), Chapter 12, of the revised statutes of 1927, being section 764.15(a),

Of Michigan Compiled Laws Annotated, and if found guilty, may subject you to not more than ninety (90) days imprisonment, and/or a fine of not more than five hundred dollars ($500.00); and, it is finally. . .

ORDERED that no security is required since neither *[Plaintiff]* nor *[Defendant]* will suffer harm from the issuance of this Injunction.

Issued on the _____ day of _____, 19___ at _____ o'clock in the _____ noon.

_____

[Circuit Judge]

A Stitch in Time Saves Nine

If there has been any physical violence between spouses during a marriage, it is then appropriate to consider protective measures regarding continued spouse abuse. An injunction is the defense against spouse abuse that is offered by the court. Penalties may be criminal or civil.

A civil spouse injunction is the least intrusive measure offered by a court. It is an order of the court which prohibits one spouse or both from harassing, harming, molesting, interfering with, assaulting, or otherwise hurting the other. A violation of a civil spouse injunction means that the perpetrator can be held in contempt of court. This can be punished by a jail sentence, a fine, or an oral reprimand not to repeat the same behavior. Obviously, a civil spouse abuse injunction is worth about as much as the paper it is written on.

Courts are generally willing to issue a spouse abuse injunction if there is a legitimate fear that there may be some harm. Usually, if there has been a past practice of spouse abuse (corroborated by police reports, hospital reports, or affidavit testimony), then a court will prefer to issue a criminal spouse abuse injunction rather than a civil spouse abuse injunction.

A criminal spouse abuse injunction is available in many states. This is an injunctive order which is similar to a civil injunction except for the fact that violation of the criminal spouse abuse injunction can carry with it a criminal conviction and possible jail sentences. Depending on the law in a jurisdiction, once a criminal injunction has been issued, a perpetrator can be arrested without a warrant merely upon the information and belief of a police officer and the report that some spouse abuse has occurred. Obviously, a criminal spouse injunction is a much more potent weapon because a mere complaint by a victim can cause an arrest.

Courts do not generally issue criminal spouse abuse injunctions without some evidence that abuse has already occurred. For example, abuse can be established by doctor or hospital reports, photographs evidencing injuries, police reports made contemporaneous with the abuse, or affidavit testimony by witnesses. All of this corroborating evidence can be presented to a judge who, based on such evidence, can issue a criminal spouse injunction. Absent such evidence, most courts would issue a civil spouse abuse injunction.

Spouse abuse injunctions can be aimed to address the misbehavior of one party or both. If a spouse injunction is mutual, it then restrains the activity of both spouses equally. Parties in a divorce should not necessarily be willing to stipulate to a mutual civil or criminal spouse abuse injunction unless there has been some past misbehavior on the separate part of each spouse. It is incorrect to assume that it does no harm to stipulate to a mutual spouse abuse injunction — whether criminal or civil. This is because a spouse abuse injunction can be used as a weapon by a vindictive spouse where no abuse has occurred.

Injunction as a Weapon

Spouse abuse injunctions can be weapons employed by an angry party. A criminal spouse abuse injunction requires a party to bring a motion before a judge requesting an order to show cause why the allegedly misbehaving spouse should not be held in contempt of court. This process is not necessarily swift.

Once a criminal spouse abuse injunction has been issued, however, in many states one spouse can complain to the police and that alone may be enough to incarcerate the other spouse. If there has been abuse, this is appropriate. Yet, if there is no abuse, then the threat of arrest can be serious for a potentially innocent spouse.

One should resist being restrained by a criminal spouse abuse injunction, particularly where there is a custody or visitation dispute. The existence of spouse abuse can be considered a factor in evaluating a custodial environment for children. A spouse who is an abuser, and against whom the court has issued a criminal spouse abuse injunction, is certainly an inappropriate candidate to be awarded child custody. Therefore, it is mandatory that you resist any effort to have a spouse abuse injunction issued (whether criminal or civil) against you because that may negatively impact your opportunities for child custody and unsupervised visitation.

Remember that a spouse abuse injunction can be used as a weapon against you; take every precaution to avoid any situation which might give rise to the issuance of such an injunction — particularly where you desire custody.

The issuance of a criminal spouse abuse injunction can certainly cause one spouse to go to jail. Sometimes a deceitful spouse will fabricate a spouse abuse scenario. While there may be no injuries, the complaining spouse can still make a police report. If you are the victim of a concoction, then it is imperative that you too make your own police report to set the facts straight according to your vantage point. Your failure to be assertive in bringing forth the facts (rather than sitting on your hands and allowing your spouse to mis-represent the situation) may send you straight to jail ... do not pass Go, do not collect $200.

A victim of spouse abuse should not hesitate to make a police report about every incident, however minor, if it constitutes harass-ment or abuse. While this may seem like petty bickering, some judges require that a substantial pattern of misbehavior be presented to the court before issuing a spouse abuse injunction. If this is your judge's approach it is imperative to complain, complain loudly, and complain quickly to the police about any abuse whether threatened, verbal, or physical. Do not let the abuse accumulate and escalate because each instance of abuse threatens to be worse than the last one.

Defend yourself by making police reports and insisting that your attorney secure an order of the court. While orders of the court are only as good as the paper they are written on, small instances of abuse can then be quickly dealt with to prevent the situation from worsening.

chapter 5 SERVING THE COMPLAINT

Hang On to Your Wallet

If you know there is an impending divorce, there is little you can do to avoid the other shoe from falling. You can wait until served with divorce papers and then reply; or, make a preemptive strike by going to an attorney, asking that the divorce filing process be accelerated, and filing your divorce complaint first. Which strategy should you choose?

If there are no assets and no issues as to alimony or children, you can wait patiently until your spouse files for divorce. Problems arise, however, when there are liquid assets in your spouse's name or in joint names, or when there are complicated or costly issues.

Assets solely in your spouses name are at risk. Your spouse can close out any bank accounts or may dispose of any assets in your spouse's sole and separate name. These assets are likely marital assets and you might be entitled to a fair share. If your spouse liquidates all the assets and sends them half-way across the United States to some out-of-state relative, a court in your state can be powerless to get your money back. This is particularly true if your spouse disappears. Then, you will be holding the short end of the financial stick.

Assets in joint names can also be at risk. For example, a joint bank account can usually be withdrawn with but one signature. With such liquid assets in joint names, letting those assets sit in the bank is about as safe as leaving money on your front lawn; don't cry in the morning when it's gone. When divorces start, love ends, and deceit begins.

To secure assets which are in your spouse's name alone, file for divorce first. Then, upon filing, obtain a property injunction *ex parte*. You alone can do nothing to protect assets in your name alone; you need the assistance of the divorce court. A judge may issue *ex parte* (that is, through a court hearing, held without any notice to your spouse, and in the absence of your spouse). This injunctive order will stop your spouse from removing those assets, selling them, concealing them, or disposing of them.

After obtaining such an *ex parte* property injunction, you must then take further action to safeguard any assets in the name of your spouse alone. This injunction must be served on every financial institutions where your spouse's assets are located; only after all such institutions have been properly serve should you notify your spouse about the injunction. By first serving the financial institution, your spouse's assets are frozen in place before your spouse has any warning of the impending divorce.

You must put the cart before the horse. First your serve the financial institutions; second, you serve your spouse. If you tell your spouse about the divorce you are going to file before the funds are frozen, then your spouse could easily go to the bank, withdraw the funds, and send the assets out-of-state. Once the money is gone, the court can order your spouse to return those assets. But that takes time. And orders of a court are just pieces of paper. If there is enough money at stake, maybe your spouse will disappear along with the cash. Then what good are a bunch of court orders?

Despite what some judge has written on a piece of paper, pieces of paper don't stop bank withdrawals unless the bank is advised ahead of time by having received an official or true copy of the divorce property injunction.

Close all joint accounts and deposit those assets in a new account in your name alone. If you are apprehensive about doing that, you can act unilaterally to freeze accounts (banks, savings and loans, money market funds, brokerage accounts, and the like). Most banks will honor a freeze by one signer on a joint account upon receipt of written notice.

If the financial institution will not freeze the account, then back to step one: shut down "Fort Knox" on your own. In protecting marital assets before filing a divorce, one of two methods is often employed: the 100% method or the 50% method.

Under the 100% method, before filing a divorce complaint, withdraw all of the money from every bank account. Open a new account and deposit every penny in that new account under your name alone. This prevents your spouse from touching those assets.

Under the 50% approach, before filing a divorce complaint, withdraw exactly one-half of the money in the joint account, redepositing your half in your name along. This gives your spouse half the pie, and you keep the remainder. This approach protects only your half of those particular cash assets.

The 100% method is preferred. This protects all assets and prevents your spouse from taking any assets without your permission or a court order. You risk losing nothing to an unscrupulous spouse. You may need both halves of these liquid, joint accounts if the court requires you to maintain the *status quo.* If you are the one required to maintain the mortgage payments, utilities, insurance, property taxes, and household living expenses during a divorce, which may carry on for several years — you may need all of the cash you can get your hand on. Don't wait for the judge to do equity ... equity helps those who help themselves.

Kidding Around

Child custody disputes may dictate that you file for divorce first if you want custody during a divorce and after a judgment is granted. The first to file can obtain an ex parte custody order for custody of the children pending a final judgment of divorce. Judges are more prone to grant permanent custody of minor children to the parent who had temporary custody while the divorce was pending.

Out of State, Out of Mind

It is important to file for divorce first when there are some assets, or issues as to alimony, or children and your spouse is out of state or you fear that they may flee the state. By filing for divorce first, you choose which state controls the proceedings.

The race to the courthouse determines where you get divorced: first in time, first in line. By allowing an out-of-state spouse to file first, you must defend a divorce from foreign shores, an undertaking both difficult and costly. Additionally, even if your spouse does not file first but leaves the state without successful service of process, then it may be painstaking to obtain jurisdiction later.

Avoiding the Inevitable

Once a divorce is filed, it is important not to avoid service of process — usually. When there is bad news, better to hear it sooner than later.

The time to avoid accepting service of process is when there are assets (to which you may have access); it is important to seize those assets before you get any (constructive or actual) notice of an injunction freezing those assets. If you are the defendant, but do not yet know whether or not the court has issued any injunctive orders (freezing your assets), then by avoiding service of process and disposing of those assets before you get notice of any injunction, you may gain control before the assets grow legs and walk.

In the end, you may have to surrender those assets or divide them as part of a settlement; but, at least there will be assets to divide. Exercise control over assets before your spouse does and they are unwittingly dissipated.

The Divorce Papers

Whenever a lawsuit is filed, the plaintiff (who files a lawsuit) must obtain jurisdiction over the defendant. Jurisdiction is obtained over a defendant when the person being sued (the defendant or respondent) is "served with papers." To be "served with papers" means that the defendant is given notice of the complaint or petition which begins the divorce proceedings as well as a summons from the court.

The summons is an official document of the court. This document is used to summon the defendant to answer the complaint for the divorce and to do so within a certain number of days. More specifically, a summons advises:

- You are being sued.

- You have a certain number of days after receiving the summons to file an answer or move to dismiss the divorce.

- If you do not answer the complaint or move to dismiss within the time allowed, a default judgment can be entered against you for the relief demanded in the complaint.

The person starting the divorce (the plaintiff or petitioner) prepares the complaint or petition. The complaint is filed with the court clerk and contains certain mandatory language. For example, the divorce complaint typically will recite:

- That the plaintiff resided in a given state and county for a certain number of days continuously, immediately preceding the filing of the complaint.

- On a certain date, the parties were married by someone legally authorized to perform marriages there.

- The wife's and husband's names prior to the marriage.

- The date when the parties separated and ceased living together as man and wife.

- Whether the wife is pregnant.

- Whether any children were born to the parties and, if so, their names and birth dates.

- That there has been a breakdown of the marriage relation ship to the extent that the objects of matrimony have been destroyed and there remains no reasonable likelihood that the marriage relationship can be preserved.

- What property the parties acquired during the marriage.

- And that a divorce is the relief being sought.

Usually, the practice of specifying a reason for the breakdown of the marriage (for example, sexual infidelity, physical abuse, lack of communication, abandonment) has either disappeared or may even be prohibited in some states. All that is legally required in most states is a vague allegation as to the breakdown of the marriage. This is called "no fault" divorce.

The summons and complaint are the two critical documents necessary to start a divorce. However, filing these documents with a court clerk and paying the necessary filing fee (usually under $100) is only enough to begin the divorce; next, the defendant or respondent must be served with the summons and complaint.

The Iceman Cometh

No divorce is granted until there is "service of process" on your spouse. That means, somehow, your spouse must be notified (in one of the legally required ways) that a divorce is pending. Your spouse is officially advised that a divorce is pending when they are "served" with the summons and complaint.

The most civil way to serve someone is to ask them to accept the summons and complaint and sign the acknowledgement of service. It is nothing more than signing a receipt for having received the document.

If your spouse will not voluntarily sign the acknowledgement of service, then more drastic measures need to be taken. Usually, there is no reason to refuse service of process, unless you need time to muster marital assets before your serves your with what might be an ex parte property injunction.

••••••••••••••••••••••••••••••••••

Ruby was a defendant who wished to torture her husband by denying him service or process. Norbert had filed for divorce and Ruby could hear the train rumbling down the tracks. Yet the light she saw at the end of the tunnel was not a ray of hope but, instead, was the train heading straight toward her. Ruby avoided service of process by going into seclusion.

Ruby and Norbert were living together when the divorce was filed. Norbert had a corporate job which took him out of the house everyday. Ruby was a homebody who principally ate bon-bons and vegetated. Once Ruby felt Norbert had filed for divorce, she stopped answering the phone, refused to acknowledge the door, and allowed no one to get within arm's reach. She shunned her mail and frustrated Norbert's every attempt to serve her with *the divorce papers.*

Norbert had only two ways to serve Ruby with *the divorce papers* since she refused to accept service of process voluntarily. First, he could effect service by mail and if that didn't work then, second, he could hire a process server (a more expensive and time-consuming proposition).

Because Ruby refused to greet the mail carrier or any other human being on the planet earth while she was engaged in her little avoidance charade, Norbert had to hire the process server.

One Saturday morning, Norbert was mulling his second cup of coffee when a young man appeared at the door. Tall, blonde haired, blue eyed, the messenger carried a small envelope from Norbert's attorney. Norbert was expecting this guest. Opening the door, he invited the young man in. Ruby, sensing another human being had passed the threshold, dashed upstairs into her bedroom, slammed the door behind her, and crawled into bed, hiding under the sheets. Ruby forgot to bolt the door to her boudoir.

Of course, it is pretty rare to have a process server give you *the divorce papers* when you are sealed beneath the sheets. Norbert and the process server hiked up the stairs in tandem, Norbert flung open the door, he walked up to the bed and yanked the sheets back, only to expose his soon-to-be-divorced wife in all of her naked glory to the process server. The young man blinked hard, twice, and tossed the summons and complaint into the bed with Ruby. She had gone to bed his wife, only to rise as his defendant.

She had barely been served with the summons and complaint when she began screaming bloody murder at the top of her lungs. The young man high-tailed it out of the bedroom, scurried down the stairs, and dashed from the house quicker than a cat on a hot tin roof. But, there is more than one way to skin a cat.

•••••••••••••••••••••••••••••••••

Another process server found it was easier to deliver the summons and complaint by using a pinch of sugar, rather than a pound of salt.

The husband and wife had been estranged for some years. While the husband knew where the wife worked, and that she had a boyfriend, he didn't know where she lived. The difficulty was, the wife worked at a federal government tank manufacturing complex.

To enter the base where the tanks were assembled, one needed a pass to get by the guard. There was no way the husband could go to where the wife worked to give her the summons and complaint. The process server was left with the creative task of trying to serve Emily.

The process server gathered together a wilted set of flowers, capturing them just before they greeted the trash heap. Leftovers from Secretaries Day. He arranged for a box and some paper used by most florists to wrap an arrangement. Inside, however, was an envelope containing *the divorce papers*. The process server found his way to the front gate of the tank automotive command.

There, security personnel refused him admission. He asked for Emily. The guard told him she was prohibited from coming to the front gate. The process server stood there forlornly, holding his trojan horse filled with "flowers."

The security guard offered to hold the flowers until Emily (or someone from her office) could come pick them up. "Oh no," the process server protested, "this is a special delivery from her boyfriend. Apparently, he wants to propose marriage. You see, what's inside the flowers is a precious diamond engagement ring. I can't leave a $4,000 arrangement at the front gate of the tank automotive command," the process server feigned.

95

The gate keeper let down his guard and became much more accommodating. The process server petitioned, "Perhaps, Emily could come out here, you could help me identify her, and then I would feel much more comfortable handing her the floral arrangement, knowing how valuable the contents are."

The guard accommodated the process server. He picked up the telephone and asked for Emily. He ordered her to appear at the front gate with I.D. in hand.

Within five minutes, Emily appeared at the front gate, clutching her identification badge. The floral delivery person asked who she was, and Emily accommodated by producing her security card. He graciously handed her the floral arrangement and said it was from a dear friend and that she should take great care to open it immediately — but only after she returned to her office.

The process server's only regret was that he missed the look on Emily's face when she opened the wilted arrangement and read the contents of the envelope — a divorce summons and complaint.

●●●●●●●●●●●●●●●●●●●●●●●●●●●●●●●●●●

Service of process often can be effected by mail. Nonetheless, a proposed defendant in a divorce will often refuse to sign the green, return-receipt card, marked *restricted delivery* at the post office, knowing that unwanted news awaits. However, there is one trick that nearly always works — particularly when used on a self-taken man.

Fred expected that his wife would file for divorce. He had plotted his disappearance some months earlier. However, he did not vanish completely because his wife still knew where Fred worked.

It wasn't hard, with a private detective, to trace that Fred was living 50 miles from work at a singles apartment complex. Apparently, Fred was getting ready for the "promised land" by positioning himself close to a spate of eligible women. Having obtained Fred's address, his wife's attorney mailed Fred a special greeting card.

The greeting card was *special* because it was an odd size, much larger than the normal special occasion card. It had a wonderfully colored, green neon envelope. Of course, there was a real greeting card inside. Something appropriate was preprinted inside like, "For you on this special day." However, taped inside of the greeting card (so it wouldn't jiggle about), was the summons and complaint. On the envelope were some of those little heart stickers, one unicorn leaping over the stars, and splashed all about the envelope was a gardenia perfume that persisted. Pleasantly scrawled across the face, in a female hand was the salutation "Freddie the Unforgettable," followed by his address. The return address was curiously absent, however, to the back of the envelope, a green, U.S. Postal Service, return-receipt card was boldly taped. Again, the female had written "Restricted delivery, to Freddie the Unforgettable."

Fred was home one Saturday morning when the mail carrier knocked on the door. Though he had been wary for months that his wife might serve him by mail, Fred just could not resist signing for that intriguingly large, colorful, aromatic card with all those pretty little hearts pounding about the envelope. Fred could hardly contain himself until the postal carrier left. He ripped open the envelope, as the mail carrier walked down the hall, safely in possession of the return receipt card. By the time the mail carrier had gone on to the next apartment building, Fred's curious excitement had soured as he read the summons and complaint. Unfortunately, he had signed for it — and that was good service of process. Fred the Elusive had become Fred the Found.

Winning by Default

Unless you are actively trying to conceal assets, it does little good to fend off service of process. The reason is this: if you won't accept service of process voluntarily, and you don't sign for your mail, and the process server can't locate you, then the court will allow *alternative* service of process.

Alternative service of process is usually accomplished by publication. A judge orders the publication of an ad in the newspaper, or nailing the summons and complaint to your front door, or mailing a copy of the complaint to you at work. Any one or more of these variations is designed to give notice of the fact that a divorce lawsuit is pending. The problem is, however, if alternative service of process is accomplished by publishing an advertisement in the paper — you may never know that a divorce was filed against you.

●●●●●●●●●●●●●●●●●●●●●●●●●●●●●●●●●●

Brian abandoned his wife. When he left town, cleaning out the house, he decided he would play hide-and-seek for a while. Brian's wife, with no children to manage and no professional job to anchor her, soon figured out Brian's "cat and mouse" game.

Though Brian never really intended to stay away too long, before he let his wife know what was going on, he "disappeared into thin air" for many months. His wife was ready to file for divorce when it became clear that Brian was nowhere to be found.

Brian's big mistake was that he left a marital home behind. Now, Brian thought he was safe because you just can't pick up a marital home and move it to Idaho. More than that, Brian thought, since the marital home was in both names, there was *no way it could be sold*. Brian's wife taught him otherwise.

Upon filing for divorce, Brian's wife notified the court that her husband, for all intents and purposes, had abandoned her and disappeared. Abandonment here constituted fault. She knew nowhere to serve him. He had quit his job, cashed out his annuity plan, and literally "flew the coup." The judge ordered alternative service by publishing a notice in the weekly newspaper over several weeks. Of course, with Brian out of town and trying to live *incognito*, he never knew a divorce was filed, and no one told him so because no one knew where he was.

After sixty days, the normal waiting period for a divorce with no children in that state, the wife was granted all of the marital assets; that's what she asked for in her complaint and, since Brian was not there to protest, he was in default. Because he was not there to defend himself, his wife was awarded her every wish.

In order to sell the marital home, the wife found a real estate broker who would pay cash (even though that meant taking a discount). The wife took the entire proceeds from the marital home and did exactly what Brian had done some months earlier — she flew the coup, disappeared, left town, and to this day Brian hasn't seen hide nor hair of her.

Moral of the Story
For Brian this was clear: Don't disappear, don't avoid service of process, don't play games! Otherwise, you might be served by publication, never get notice, and lose whatever joint assets you may have.

Sample Divorce Complaint

Federal courts have no jurisdiction over divorces. However, each state does have its own laws regarding divorce. Similarly, the form of a divorce complaint will vary among the states. Many states require by law that certain language be included in every divorce complaint; this is called statutory language.
The following sample divorce complaint derives from Michigan.[2]
It is offered merely as an example.

2 See *Michigan Divorce Manual* by Thomas Oehmke (1986 West Publishing Company, St. Paul, Minn.).

State of Michigan
[County] **County Circuit Court**

[Plaintiff],   Case No. *[Number]*
         Plaintiff
vs.   Hon. *[Judge]*
         Circuit Judge
[Defendant],
         Defendant

[Attorney]
Attorney for Plaintiff
[Street Address]
[City], *[State]* *[Zip]*
[Phone]

COMPLAINT FOR DIVORCE
Verification

NOW COMES *[Plaintiff]* Plaintiff, through the law firm of *[Attorney]* and in support of this Complaint for Divorce, says:

1. That *[Plaintiff]* Plaintiff has resided in the State of Michigan for at least 180, and the County of *[County]* for at least 10 days, continuously, immediately preceding the filing of this Complaint.

2. That on *[Date]*, the parties were legally married by *[Person]*, who was legally authorized to solemnize the marriage, and did so at *[Place]*.

3. That the wife's name prior to this marriage was *[Name]*.

4. That *[Plaintiff]* and *[Defendant]* separated on or about *[Date]*.

5.That during this marriage, and up to the date of filing this Complaint, *[Plaintiff]* and *[Defendant]* gave birth to the following child[ren] on the stated date(s) of birth, namely: *[Child's]*, born on *[Date]*.

6.That the Plaintiff desires temporary and permanent custody of the minor children and that Plaintiff is a fit and proper person to be awarded such custody.

7.That Plaintiff is without sufficient funds to support the minor children of the parties, and Defendant should be ordered to pay temporary and permanent support for the minor children of the parties, all necessary medical, dental, hospital expenses, and maintain hospitalization insurance for the minor children of the parties, until each child attains the age of eighteen (18), or until further order of this Court.

8.That the minor children presently reside with *[Custodian]* in *[County]* County, at *[Street Address, City, State]*. Other than this address, and during the past five years, the minor children have resided at the following address(es): *[Street Address, City, State]*.

9.That Plaintiff has not participated as a party in other divorce litigation concerning the custody of the minor children of the parties (nor does Plaintiff know of a person not a party to the proceedings who has physical custody of the minor children of the parties or claims to have custody or visitation rights with respect to the minor children of the parties).

10.That there has been a breakdown in the marriage relationship to the extent that the objects of matrimony have been destroyed and there remains no reasonable likelihood that the marriage relationship can be preserved.

11.That while *[Plaintiff]* and *[Defendant]* lived and cohabited together as husband and wife, certain marital property was acquired, and *[Plaintiff]* should be awarded an equitable share of said property.

12. That *[Plaintiff]* is without sufficient funds to maintain the household and daily expenses, and seeks a temporary and permanent order of alimony; and further, that *[Defendant]* is well able to contribute to the needs of *[Plaintiff]*.

13. That *[Plaintiff]* is without sufficient funds to pay attorney fees, and further, that *[Defendant]* is capable of paying said fees.

14. That *[Plaintiff]* has been subjected to the physical abuse of *[Defendant]*, including, but not limited to the following: on or about *[Date]*, *[Defendant]* did *[Specify Act(s)]*. Further, that *[Plaintiff]* fears said actions will continue unless *[Defendant]* is restrained by an order of the Court.

15. That *[Defendant]* has threatened to sell, destroy, or otherwise dispose of the property of the parties, including, but not limited to the following: on or about *[Date]*, *[Defendant]* did *[Specify Act(s)]*. Further, that *[Plaintiff]* is fearful of irreparable harm and loss unless *[Defendant]* and any agent(s) are restrained by order of this Court.

WHEREFORE, *[Plaintiff]* requests:

A. That *[Defendant]* answer this Complaint for Divorce under oath.

B. That the marriage between *[Plaintiff]* and *[Defendant]* be dissolved and a divorce from the bonds of matrimony be decreed to *[Plaintiff]*, according to the statutes.

C.That *[Plaintiff]* be awarded an equitable share of the marital property.

D.That a temporary and permanent order be entered against *[Defendant]* to maintain the household expenses of *[Plaintiff]*, and to pay a reasonable amount of alimony for the support of *[Plaintiff]*.

E.That *[Defendant]* be ordered to pay to the attorney for *[Plaintiff]*, a reasonable attorney fee.

F.   That a domestic abuse injunction be issued (pursuant to MCL 552.14 or, alternatively, MCL 764.15(a)) prohibiting *[Defendant]* from assaulting, molesting, beating, or wounding *[Plaintiff]*.

G.That an order be issued restraining *[Defendant]* from selling, assigning, transferring, or otherwise disposing of the property of the parties.

H.That the Wife's name be restored to *[Name]*, which was her name before this marriage.

I.That the temporary and permanent custody of the minor children of the parties be awarded to *[Plaintiff]*.

J.That *[Defendant]* be ordered to pay temporary and permanent support for the support of the minor children of the parties, plus all medical, dental, hospital expenses, as well as maintain hospitalization insurance for the minor children.

K.That this Court grant *[Plaintiff]* further relief as may be just and equitable.

_____   Dated: *[Date]*

[Attorney]
Attorney for Plaintiff

AFFIDAVIT
VERIFICATION OF PLEADING

In the State of Michigan, County of *[County]*, *[Plaintiff]*, Affiant, makes this oath or affirmation, being duly sworn, deposes and says that:

1. I am the Plaintiff named in the above-captioned matter and, as such, have knowledge of the fact(s) pleaded.

2. I have read the above Complaint for Divorce and the statements contained in such pleading(s) are stated positively or on information and belief according to the facts; moreover, any such pleading is not interposed for delay.

3. I declare under penalty of contempt of court that to the best of my knowledge, information, and belief there is good ground to support the contents of such pleading(s).

[Plaintiff]
Affiant

Subscribed and sworn to before me on *[Date]*.

[Notary Public]
[County] County, *[State]*
Commission Expires: *[Date]*

chapter 6 GOING TO TRIAL

Mediation

One alternative to resolving contested divorce issues through a judge trial begins with mediation. In some instances, mediation is mandatory and court ordered. Other times, it is voluntary. Mediation can be an effective alternative dispute resolution mechanism where there are substantial marital assets, where values are disputed, where liabilities abound, or where there are issues of fault.

Mediation is a non-binding procedure usually conducted by one attorney. It occurs in the mediator's office. Customarily, a mediation summary is drafted (much like a term paper) which sets forth the parties' respective positions on custody, support, visitation, alimony, and property distribution. The mediation summary also lists assets with associated values and suggests an equitable division of the property.

Using shuttle diplomacy and jaw-boning, a mediator can usually give the parties a sense as to how a trial judge would decide their issues. A mediator can persuade reluctant clients and stubborn attorneys to settle matters which are careening toward trial.

An effective mediator will have 15 years or more experience in divorce practice and should boast a few gray hairs for the sake of credibility. The mediator will often take from three hours to an entire day or more in resolving issues.

At the conclusion of mediation, the parties should enter into a written agreement which memorializes how the issues have been resolved. Many judges will urge the parties to come to court right from the mediator's office and place a settlement on the record, if that has been achieved.

Because mediation takes perhaps 20% of the time that a normal trial would take, you should urge your attorney to consider this method of alternative dispute resolution if it seems like your spouse or spouse's attorney is being unreasonable.

Arbitration[3]

Arbitration is the similar to mediation. Mediators suggest *non-binding* recommendations to settle a divorce; differently, arbitrators make *final and binding* decisions which, like it or not, resolve the dispute. In mediation, there must be concurrence to settle an issue (both parties must agree); a mediator has no power to force a settlement — except the power of persuasion. An arbitrator, on the other hand, is a private judge retained by the parties to decide the unresolved issues.

Arbitration offers speed, economy, and privacy. It is a fast process because parties are not bogged down by cumbersome rules of evidence and procedural restraints. It is a more economic process than litigating because it is quicker and is done in an informal setting of the arbitrator's office, without the delays normally associated with going to trial. It is private because no one is allowed to observe the process; your "dirty laundry" is washed behind closed doors and out of public view. The outcome of the arbitration proceeding is private, except to the extent that it might be reduced to a judgment of divorce (which is a public document).

3 See *Commercial Arbitration* by Thomas Oehmke (1987 Clark Boardman Callahan, Rochester, New York), supplemented annually.

The American Arbitration Association (AAA) is the premier national association offering arbitration services. Offices are located in all metropolitan centers. However, the parties need not go through AAA to choose an arbitrator; any person may be chosen by the parties as an arbitrator. Arbitrators are privately compensated by the parties for their time. Because arbitration is quicker than litigation, the extra fees paid to an arbitrator are usually much less than even your own attorney fees would be, if compelled to litigate.

If your case involves complex issues regarding custody, fault, or property distribution, arbitration should be considered as an alternative dispute resolution method, offering speed, economy, and privacy.

The Name Game

In the most marriages, it is customary for a woman to take her husband's last name. Of course, there are many instances today where a wife retains her name and some instances where a woman hyphenates her name and that of her husband.

Deborah was married to John and, as was the custom, chose John's last name. It was a good last name politically as well as in the legal community. Both Deborah and John were attorneys. The couple's last name (we'll just say that it was "Hathaway" for discussion's sake) was a good political name because John's mother was a prominent state supreme court judge. Everyone had known Judge Hathaway for her integrity and years of service on the bench.

Regrettably, John and Deborah's marriage did not have the same longevity as Judge Hathaway's judicial career. After six months, the parties sought a divorce and it was quickly granted because there was no property dispute and no children. About the same time, John's mother was retiring from the bench.

Deborah coveted the idea of serving as a judge. During the course of the divorce, with her then mother-in-law's impending retirement from the judiciary a matter of public interest, Deborah filed her petition to become the successor to her then mother-in-law, Judge Hathaway.

As is too often the case in judicial elections, the candidate's name overshadows judicial qualifications. Indeed, Deborah Hathaway running for the vacant seat created by her former mother-in-law, Judge Hathaway, had an excellent chance of being elected — but only because her last name was Hathaway.

In the course of the divorce, Deborah elected to keep the name Hathaway (even though she had been only briefly married to John). In the state where they were divorced, a circuit judge may allow a woman to change her name when a divorce is granted. The woman may request that she be restored her birth name, the surname she legally bore prior to her marriage, or another surname — provided the change is not sought with fraudulent or evil intent. Given these options, Deborah fancied the last name Hathaway, particularly given her judicial ambitions.

John argued steadfastly to the divorce judge that Deborah should not be allowed to keep *his* name, as if the name he had so freely surrendered was precious personal property. In fact, John actually wanted to run for his mother's judicial seat but two Hathaways on the ballot would have muddied the waters. Since Deborah chose to keep the last name Hathaway, the court allowed her to do so. She ran for judge and was elected. John never filed to run for election. And, as it occurred, Deborah Hathaway turned out to be a fine judge (despite her chosen name).

Moral of the Story
Once you give away your name in marriage, you can't take it back. And if you don't like the name you've taken, most states will allow you to change that name back to your birth name or any other name that is not meant to deceive or confuse your identify.

Soldiers and Sailors

Many states have passed a "Soldiers and Sailors Relief Act." This state legislation suspends divorce proceedings involving enlisted personnel or officers in active duty military service. Indeed, all lawsuits (including divorces) stand adjourned until after a soldier or sailor ends their active duty service unless they voluntarily consent to the lawsuit moving forward. Therefore, in a state where such a law has been passed, no judgment of divorce can be obtained against any person unless the plaintiff can demonstrate to the court by affidavit that the defendant is not in the military.

If service of process has been obtained (a summons and complaint having been served) on a person who is in active duty military service, and the defendant does not reply to such lawsuit and a default is filed, courts — in states where such a statute has been passed — will not enter a judgment of divorce until it can be established that the defendant is not in the active duty military.

Taking a *Pro Con*

To take a *pro confesso* (or *pro con*) divorce means to go before the court and testify why a divorce should be granted. Some people refer to this as going to court to "get a divorce." This process can be abbreviated. It is much like a small candle on top of a very elaborate cake. By the time you go to court, the cake is baked: all of the property has been divided, custody is determined, visitation is arranged, alimony decided, and all the pieces are in place. The *pro con* merely "blows the candle out."

There is no doubt that it often takes longer to ride the elevator in the courthouse than it does to actually stand in front of the judge and "get a divorce." The questioning in court typically goes as follows:

"Smith v Smith, Case No. 99-123456-DM," the clerk summons, announcing your case.

You and your attorney then scurry to the front of the courtroom and stand before the judge. "Raise your right hand," the clerk orders. You then raise your left hand and the clerk will remind you to raise the "other right hand." Your attorney will ask the question and you will answer:

Q. *Do you swear or affirm that you will tell the truth, the whole truth, and nothing but the truth?*

A. *I do.*

Q. *Please state your name for the record.*

A. *I am the Plaintiff, Pete Doe.*

Q. *Were all of the allegations in your divorce complaint true when you filed the complaint and are they still true today?*

A. *Yes.*

Q. *Are you on public assistance or are you expecting a child?*

A. *No.*

Q. *Has there been a breakdown of the marriage relationship to the extent that the objects of matrimony have been destroyed and there*

> *remains no reasonable likelihood that the marriage can be preserved?*

A.   *Yes.*

Usually, that's all there is to it. Some judges will require more information, few will require less.

If there has been a default filed because your spouse, though served with divorce papers, has refused to answer, you may have to identify your spouse's signature. Your spouse may have signed for the post office return-receipt of a summons and complaint or may even have stipulated in writing to the form of the divorce judgment. However, you may still have to identify your spouse's signature. This provides some corroborating evidence that your spouse has been placed on notice about this divorce.

Once the *pro con* hearing is concluded, a written judgment of divorce is signed by the judge. A sample of such default judgment follows.

Sample Divorce JudgmentSample Divorce Judgment
>   State of Michigan
>   [County] County Circuit Court

[Plaintiff],   Case No. [Number]
>   Plaintiff
vs.   Hon. [Judge]
>   Circuit Judge
[Defendant],
>   Defendant

[Attorney]
Attorney for Plaintiff
[Street Address]
[City], [State] [Zip]
[Phone]

[Attorney]
Attorney for Defendant
[Street Address]
[City], [State] [Zip]
[Phone]

Default Judgment of Divorce

At a session of said Court
held in the chambers of
the above referenced Judge on

PRESENT: Hon. [Judge]
Circuit Judge

This cause having been brought on to be heard upon Plaintiff's Complaint for Divorce, taken as confessed by Defendant, and the proofs having been presented in open Court, from which it satisfactorily appears that there has been a breakdown in the marriage relationship to the extent that the objects of matrimony have been destroyed and there remains no reasonable likelihood that the marriage can be preserved, and that Plaintiff is entitled to the relief prayed for:

Therefore, on motion of [Attorney], Attorney for [Plaintiff], Plaintiff, the Court enters its Judgment as follows:

Divorce

ORDERED that the marriage of the parties shall be, and hereby is, dissolved and that the parties are hereby divorced from the bonds of matrimony; and, it is further adjudged and

Alimony

ORDERED that neither party be awarded alimony; further, this provision shall settle all rights to alimony for all time, and neither party shall be entitled to file any subsequent petition for alimony;

Dower

ORDERED that the [Plaintiff], Plaintiff and [Defendant], Defendant shall retain whatever personal property is now in their respective possessions, free and clear of any claim on the part of the other (including all vehicles, household goods, bank accounts, pension plans, stocks and bonds, accumulated during the marriage and not otherwise disposed of by this Judgment of Divorce);

ORDERED that this property settlement is a provision made for each of the parties in lieu of dower in the lands of the other and, further, each shall hereafter hold the remaining lands free and clear and discharged from any such dower right or claim of the other;

Insurance provision

ORDERED that any rights of either party in any policy or contract of life, endowment or annuity insurance, are hereby extinguished, unless reserved specifically elsewhere in this Judgment;

Child Custody

ORDERED that both parties shall maintain joint custody and responsibility for the care, maintenance, and education of the minor children. Each party shall devote an equal amount of time and effort with the children toward those ends;

ORDERED that [Party] be granted the physical custody of these minor children until age eighteen (18), or further order of the Court, namely, [Child's Name], and shall then be solely responsible for financing the food, housing, clothing, and other necessaries (except for medical care) of the children, while the non custodial parent shall pay child support toward these ends, as ordered below;

Child Support

ORDERED that [Defendant], Defendant shall pay in advance to the [Plaintiff], Plaintiff through the Friend of the Court, for the benefit of the minor children, the sum of $ .00 per child per week, until each child becomes 18 years of age or graduates from high school (whichever comes later), or until further order of the Court;

Back Temporary Support

ORDERED that all back child support (or alimony, if any) which is owing as of the date of this Judgment be paid forthwith;

Service Fee

ORDERED that [Defendant], Defendant shall pay to the Friend of the Court the sum of $2.00 per month, payable semi annually in advance on January 1 and July 1, while the Judgment for Child Support is operative. Payments for the next coming January 1 or July 1 shall be made immediately;

Child Visitation

ORDERED that [Plaintiff], Plaintiff shall have physical custody of the children, while [Defendant], Defendant shall have reasonable visitation privileges, as mutually agreed between the parties and the minor children.

In addition to these reasonable visitation privileges, [Defendant], Defendant shall also visit with the children from [Time] until [Time] on every other of the following holidays or weekends:

New Year's Eve/New Year's Day
Memorial Day weekend
Independence Day
Labor Day weekend
Thanksgiving Day/Friday after Thanksgiving and weekend
Passover/Easter Holidays
Hanukkah/Christmas Eve

Further, [Defendant], Defendant shall have said children for [Number] week[s] during the summer, [Defendant] giving [Plaintiff] 30 days written notice of the desired visitation period; and [Defendant] shall promptly return the children to [Plaintiff] at the end of the visit;

Health Care for Minor Child[ren]

ORDERED that [Defendant], Defendant pay the reasonable and necessary medical, dental and hospital expenses of the minor children until each becomes 18 years old or until further order of the Court;

Change of Domicile

ORDERED that the domicile or residence of the minor child(ren) shall not be removed from the State of Michigan without the approval of the Judge who awarded custody, or any successor, and both [Plaintiff] and [Defendant] shall promptly notify the Friend of the Court in writing of any change of address for themself, or of any minor child, until all minor children have reached the age of 18.

The present address of said children is in [County] County at [Street Address, City, State, Zip].

Personal Property

ORDERED that all personal property, presently owned by the respective parties, in their individual names, shall remain their sole and separate properties, free from any right, title or claim by the other party;

ORDERED that [Party] shall execute: (a) a bill of sale transferring all of h/her right, title and interest in and to the household goods and furniture of these parties located at [Street Address, City, State, Zip]; and, (b) an assignment of certificate of title, No. [Number], covering a [Year, Make Model and Vehicle Identification Number (VIN)] automobile, together with the discharge of the lien recited in the said certificate of title transferring said automobile to [Opposing Party];

Real Property

ORDERED that the [Party] shall execute: (a) the quit claim deed conveying all of [Party's] right, title and interest in [Describe Property] commonly known as [Street Address, City, State, Zip] subject to the existing mortgage held by [Mortgagee];

Other Property

ORDERED that any rights of either party in any pension or policy or contract of life, endowment or annuity insurance, Individual Retirement Account (IRA), and Simplified Employee Pension (SEP), or any other benefit in which the opposing party is named as beneficiary, are hereby extinguished, unless specifically elsewhere in this Judgment;

ORDERED that all personal and other property not otherwise listed above and presently in the possession of each of the parties, shall remain their respective sole and separate property, free from any right, title, or claim by the other;

ORDERED that [Party] shall assume responsibility for all mortgage and escrow (insurance, taxes, and the like) payments for the above referenced property and shall indemnify and hold [Opposing Party] harmless from all such payments;

Recordation of Judgment

ORDERED that each party shall execute, acknowledge and deliver to each other, as and when required, any and all deeds, bills of sale, documents, stock certificates, stock transfer powers, assignments, insurance applications, titles, and/or other documents of ownership or title or instruments of release, assurance, assignment, transfer or conveyance, in order to effectuate the terms and provisions hereof;

ORDERED that, in the event either party shall fail, refuse or neglect to execute, acknowledge and deliver any instrument required to implement the terms and provisions of this Judgment of Divorce, then and in that event, said Judgment shall be self executing and shall stand in the place and stead of any of the instruments required hereunder; further, a certified copy of this Judgment of Divorce may be recorded with any register of deeds, Secretary of State, stock transfer agent, or other public office thereto to have the same force and effect as if such instrument had, in fact, been executed;

Retention of Jurisdiction

ORDERED that this Court retains jurisdiction over this cause and the parties to assuring compliance with the executory provisions of this Judgment and this Court reserves the right to make such further consistent orders as necessary to implement this Judgment;

Attorney Fees

ORDERED that [Defendant], Defendant shall pay [Amount] to [Plaintiff]'s attorney as attorney's fees and costs; one half of such payment shall be made within 45 days and the balance within 90 days of the date of this order;

ORDERED that each party is to pay all other fees and costs of this litigation;

Restoration of Name

ORDERED that the Wife's prior name of [Name] is restored;

Income Withholding

ORDERED that, pursuant to MCL ' 514.12 and MCL ' 513.22(4), in the event a delinquency in the support account exists, upon proper notice an assignment of income shall issue;

ORDERED that, pursuant to MCL ' 513.22(10), [Defendant], Defendant shall give the office of the Friend of the Court the name and address of any present and future employer;

ORDERED that, pursuant to MCL ' 513.22(11), this order of income withholding shall be binding upon any source of income for [Defendant] upon seven days after service upon that source of income by ordinary mail of a copy of the support order entered herein and a true copy of this order of income withholding, which shall remain in effect until further order of the Court;

Permanent Injunction

ORDERED that [Defendant], Defendant is forever barred from assaulting, molesting, harassing, and interfering with the personal liberty of [Plaintiff], Plaintiff.

_____

[Judge]

Stipulation to/Waiver of Entry of Order

☐ I stipulate to the entry of this above Order [under MCR 2.119(D)(2)(a)].

☐ Notice and hearing on entry of the above Order is waived [under MCR 2.119(D)(2)(b)].

_____   _____
[Attorney]   [Plaintiff]
Attorney for [Plaintiff]

_____   _____
[Attorney]   [Defendant]
Attorney for [Defendant]

It's Not Over When It's Over

A divorce is over when a judgment is entered either by default (because the defendant did not come to court and defend), by consent (which means both parties have agreed to all the terms of the judgment), or by order of the court (after a trial). Once a judgment is entered, the divorce is concluded.

However, just because a divorce judgment has been entered, the issues are not necessarily ended forever. Certain disputes can be reopened by the court years after the final judgment has been granted.

Child support is an issue that can be revisited periodically. Customarily, the court may adjust child support every several years, though local custom varies. However, a change in circumstances allows child support to be decreased (if the child support payor has a substantial reduction in income) or increased (if the needs of the children have increased and there is a corresponding ability to pay on the part of the obligated parent). Child support is modified when one party brings a motion to modify the judgment of divorce with regard to support.

Child visitation is an issue that can be modified after a divorce judgment has been entered. Child visitation issues can be reopened until a child reaches the age of majority. Visitation can be expanded, contracted, eliminated, or regulated depending on the needs of the parents and the best interests of the child.

Residence of the child can be effected by the court in the context of custody. While citizens have a constitutional right to free travel, many states prohibit a custodial parent from removing the children from the state where the divorce is granted without permission of the court.

The court's leverage to regulate residency of a child whose custodial parent is leaving the state is to transfer custody to the parent who remains, if that is in the best interests of the child. This long-arm of the law not only assures reasonable visitation for the non-custodial parent without long-distance travel requirements, but it assures that the custodial parent will not punish the other parent by removing the children so that visitation is effectively barred.

Alimony may be modified assuming it has been granted or reserved in the divorce judgment. If alimony was not initially granted, a court normally has the implied right to grant alimony at a later date. However, as a practical matter, when alimony is initially denied, the judgment usually provides that alimony is forever barred.

Alimony could also be declared to be open, reserved, closed forever, or subject to reconsideration. To prevent doubt, alimony should be addressed in the judgment specifically by stating whether or not it can be revisited.

Enforcing the judgment is another basis for the court to retain continuing jurisdiction. For example, if one party was to have transferred an asset to another party but fails to do so, the court maintains continuing jurisdiction to enforce its judgments. This allows the spouse who was short-changed to return to the divorce judge and complain.

The court rules of some states may allow a judgment to be reopened within a limited period of time (usually one year) after being granted. Reasons to reopen a judgment may include fraud, misrepresentation, or some other deception which was not known when the original judgment was granted.

To be clear, once a divorce judgment is signed by the judge, even if you don't like it, you are probably going to have to live with it. If you agree (either by stipulation in writing or orally before the court) to certain provisions being included in a divorce judgment, you will be bound by them.

Before agreeing to any provision in a judgment of divorce, read each word carefully and be sure you understand what those words mean. If you don't understand them, there is no such thing as a stupid question. Ask your attorney. Play dumb. Learn what you don't know. Make sure that you can explain every provision of your divorce judgment to a ten year old child (if asked). If you don't understand what that judgment says, there is no time like the present to learn. In fact, if you don't figure it out before the judgment is entered, you will live with the consequences, no matter how undesirable. Speak now, or forever hold your peace.

An Appealing End to Things

If a divorce judgment is entered by default (because the defendant has failed to appear and defend the case), there is usually no appeal. The exception, which allows an appeal from a default judgment is that you were never properly given notice that a divorce had been filed against you.

If you fail to answer a complaint for divorce and defend, you cannot complain later if your spouse "takes you to the cleaners." It is totally permitted for one married person to file a divorce and ask the court to award them all of the assets. If your spouse has filed for divorce and you do not defend the action, you could be deprived of all the assets and awarded the liabilities. Therefore, do not sit on your hands once a divorce has been filed against you. Immediately seek the advice of counsel -- unless there are no assets, no liabilities, no children, and no request for alimony. Otherwise, caveat emptor.

If a divorce has been entered by consent, and both parties have signed the judgment, there is usually no appeal, absent fraud or misrepresentation.

The only time a divorce judgment can be appealed is if disputed issues are decided by a judge who renders a judgment. Usually, the issues most frequently appealed are those of child custody, property division, and alimony. To appeal, however, one must have made a good record with facts and witnesses before a trial judge. An appeal is on the record and based upon the evidence actually presented, not what you wish you could have presented but failed to.

Rushing Back to the Altar

Some states have no minimum waiting period before remarriage; in those states, you can remarry the same day you are divorced.

Unless getting remarried to each other, some other states do have a minimum period before one can remarry. Waiting periods range from 60 days to 2 years, or sooner at the court's discretion. Sometimes, the waiting period only applies in cases of adultery (or, in one state, where the wife was a prostitute before marriage).

In cases of adultery, a defendant can be barred from marriage to anyone (other than the plaintiff) during the plaintiff's lifetime; or, defendant can be barred from marrying the co-respondent during the plaintiff's lifetime.

At any rate, before rushing back to the altar, learn if there is some minimum waiting period.

chapter 7 FAULT MEANS MONEY

Equitable is Not Always Equal

There are no mathematical formulas which govern the distribution of property in a divorce action. No rigid rule instructs as to who gets what property. The divorce judgment need not *equally* divide marital property, but it must do so *equitably*.

When making an equitable division of the marital estate, a divorce court usually considers:

- Duration of the marriage.
- Contributions of both parties to the joint estate.
- Parties' stations in life.
- Parties' earning abilities.
- Fault or past misconduct.
- Parties' respective ages.
- Parties' health.
- Other pertinent circumstances.
- Necessities of life for each party.

- Adequacy of child support alone to provide necessaries for minor children.
- Other equitable circumstances.

All of these considerations will be weighed by the court in making an equitable distribution of the marital estate. Yet, despite these factors, the court usually makes an equal 50/50 split of the assets, unless there is serious fault.

The Secret Lover

Most states recognize the concept of "fault" in the context of divorce. That is, if your spouse has been at fault for the breakdown of the marriage — even in so-called "no fault" states — then fault can be important to property division.

Regardless of fault, a divorce can be granted (as long as there has been a breakdown of marriage to the extent that the objects of matrimony have been destroyed and there is no reasonable likelihood that the marriage can be preserved). Thus, if one party wants a divorce, regardless of how the other party objects, the divorce is usually granted. However, that is not the end of the story as to property issues.

•••••••••••••••••••••••••••••••••

Richard, the defendant, was a trial judge. His wife of many years had long suspected his involvement in extra-marital affairs. However, Richard was more discrete than his wife was persistent. While Richard, indeed, had carried on his affairs, his wife could never prove what she knew in her "heart of hearts."

During the divorce, Richard's wife, Sylvia, pressed the issue of marital infidelity. She contended that Richard's unfaithfulness had caused the breakdown of the marriage. However, Sylvia had no objective proof and feelings and subjective belief are inadmissible and prove nothing.

Whitney

Richard had never used any credit card for an indiscrete expense. He had never been "caught with his pants down" by a detective-for-hire photographer. There was no "co-respondent" who came forward to confess that she was the object of Richard's desire. In the end, there was nothing more than raw suspicion — as well founded in Sylvia's instinct as it might have been.

The matter went to trial because no property settlement was reached. By then, the children were grown and the last issue, to which Sylvia clutched desperately, was the division of the substantial marital estate. If Sylvia could prove that Richard had been "at fault" (because of long term infidelity), Sylvia could take the lioness's share of the marital estate. Sylvia's attorney called Richard, "His Honor," to the stand for questioning:

> **Q.** *Have you ever been involved in any extra-marital affair?*
>
> **A.** *My wife, my wife, she has been quite an affair over the years. But, extra? Extra in what respect? Extra in the respect of someone in addition to Sylvia? Now exactly, how do you mean that?*
>
> **Q.** *Sir, let us be frank. During the years that you were married to Sylvia, did you ever have sexual intercourse with any other woman?*
>
> **A.** *I invoke the Fifth Amendment on the grounds that the answer I give may tend to incriminate me.*

Now that was straight-forward and took the judge off guard. It is one thing to beat around the bush, but quite another, however, to be that frank.

Outraged, Sylvia's attorney leapt to his feet. "He might as well admit adultery, taking the Fifth Amendment!" the wife's attorney blustered.

The divorce judge looked at the witness and turned to the wife's counsel. "It is one thing to take the Fifth Amendment, but another to admit adultery. Taking the Fifth Amendment is not an admission. To confess adultery would be an admission to a crime in this state. Silence is not proof that there has been adultery committed by the husband. I cannot conclude that there has been. Now then, because the witness takes the Fifth Amendment, we will move along to the next subject," the divorce judge resolved. And that was that.

Cleverly, Richard had not admitted to adultery. Neither, had the wife proven any adulteress behavior. In the end, there was an equal division of the divorce assets, because the wife did not establish — by a preponderance of the evidence — that the husband had committed adultery.

A preponderance of the evidence means that, based on the evidence admitted at trial, there was a 51% possibility that the husband had committed adultery. But here, there was no proof of facts. There was the wife's accusation and the husband's refusal to admit or deny. The judge awarded an equal division of the assets, lacking objective proof, there being no evidence of adultery.

Moral of the Story

It is one thing to invoke the Fifth Amendment, but it's an entirely different matter to confess to adultery. Don't do it. What your spouse knows in their "heart of hearts" may be entirely different than what your spouse can prove by objective evidence in a court of law. Don't count on your spouse to confess adultery on the witness stand in divorce court. Better to believe in miracles.

"No Fault" Means Fault

Even in states with "no fault" divorce laws, the concept of

fault often controls aspects of the divorce proceedings.

"No fault" was conceived to eliminate the factual disputes arise about who has been at fault for having caused the breakdown of the marriage. Under common law, a marriage could not be dissolved unless the defendant had caused the breakdown of the marriage. This sometimes led to naming some non-existent co-respondent or co-defendant. Co-respondents were named as the "other woman" or "other man" who had engaged in a tryst with the defendant, "causing" the breakdown of the marriage. Over the years, the co-respondent and other fictions led to such perjury that the fault requirement has been widely abolished.

The fact that fault has been more or less eradicated when deciding whether or not to grant a divorce does not mean that it has been eliminated from the process. If one can establish fault and simultaneously show one's own "clean hands," then the innocent spouse may lay claim to a greater piece of the marital pie.

A variety of factors can constitute fault, including marital infidelity, financial gross recklessness, concealment of a known and material physical or mental impairment, opposite notions about having children, and similar problems.

To establish fault, you must do so by admissible evidence. Such evidence may include photographs, expert testimony, witnesses, tape recordings, and the like. One must be particularly careful about using tape recordings to trap a misbehaving spouse; some states make such "wire-tapping" lawful where one party to a conversation consents; however, other states prohibit such electronic eavesdropping. Where you do not participate in a telephone conversation, most state and federal laws may convert your tape-recording into the crime of wire-tapping.

Even where fault can be proven by a preponderance of the evidence, the reward is questionable. Some judges, when persuaded that there has been substantial fault on the part of one party alone, may award disproportionate shares of the marital estate. The innocent spouse may receive 55% or more of the marital estate, while the party at fault receives the remainder. In larger cities and more liberal jurisdictions, progressive-minded judges are reticent to award any premium to the innocent spouse who may be a victim of their partner's fault. To be sure, fault should not be ignored, but it should be used more as a bargaining lever for a better settlement.

Drugs, Booze, and Beatings

Common complaints with regard to fault are substance (drugs and/or alcohol) abuse, and physical abuse. Some spouses legitimately complain about long-term marriages which have involved such trauma. While such spouse abuse is important in proving fault, the corollary of "clean hands" by an innocent spouse must also be introduced.

The misbehavior of your spouse is usually not punished by the court rewarding you extra assets as the innocent spouse if you have "chosen" to remain in the marital relationship. The "voluntary nature" of your remaining in an abusive relationship is the subject of much psychological debate. Many victims of spouse abuse or alcoholic partners do not *voluntarily* remain in the relationship, even though the abuse may have persisted for years.

Without debating the psychology of being trapped in a relationship which victimizes an innocent spouse, many courts are often hesitant to "reward" the innocent spouse with a greater share of the marital estate. Of course, there may be an initial period when an innocent spouse endures an abusive relationship short-term in the hope of rehabilitating he abuser. However, when all good faith efforts have been exhausted and it appears that there can be no rehabilitation of an abusive spouse, thereafter, the courts are unlikely to be sympathetic to the victim who continues in a relationship for a substantial number of years thereafter.

Rather than seek a disproportionate share of marital assets, a sometimes successful approach is to attempt to itemize the economic impact of the abusive conduct. For example, if the offending spouse is a gambler, and has wagered unsuccessfully and you can calculate the amount of the gambling loss, then a financial analysis might be done. By calculating the drain of marital assets over a period of years spent on gambling — particularly where this has been done in a secretive manner without the innocent spouse's consent — one can quantify the request for a larger share of marital assets. If the innocent spouse can prove that $50,000 of marital assets was wasted over 10 years on a gambling addiction, the innocent spouse may seek one-half of the dissipated marital assets plus interest. This is a cost-detriment analysis of marital misbehavior.

Act timely to preserve marital assets where all good faith efforts have been exhausted in an attempt to rehabilitate a spouse who is wasting away the marital estate. Seek the protection of the court (either by a divorce decree or a separate maintenance decree) preventing marital assets from being dissipated. Once assets are gone, they're gone! Do not pray for a sympathetic divorce judge to reward the tardy spouse who ignores the assistance of the court. God helps those who help themselves.

The Burning Bed Cure

Where an abusive relationship is protracted, some victims ultimately muster enough moral strength to rectify the situation. Television and movies have depicted their fare with the "burning bed" defense. That is, where a spouse (usually the husband) has so abused the wife for a number of years that she cannot take the abuse any longer, she defends herself by burning the bed (with him in it) and terminating the abusive situation. Clearly illegal and not a desirable remedy — particularly if you are the husband! There is another approach.

Instead of burning the bed, you could withdraw all the bank accounts, pack your bags, load the kids in the back of the car, and leave the state. That is provided that you have sufficient marital assets to be able to relocate and start up on your own. There is nothing illegal about cleaning out the bank accounts and leaving the state with the children to set up a new domicile, particularly in self-defense when caught in an abusive relationship. Of course, you cannot intend to kidnap your own children in violation of the Federal Parental Kidnapping Act. But, with a clear conscience and good intent, you may defend yourself by leaving the abusive situation for self-protective reasons.

This is not the most desirable approach if your spouse locates you. However, it is an improvement over serving a life sentence for felony murder and effectively "orphaning" your children.

If you insist on being "fair," take only your equal share. But, leaving town might be the most expeditious solution to a bad situation. You could call it the geographic cure.

chapter 8 THE MARITAL HOME

Moving by Remote Control

Some people are not very good at personal relationships. Of course, those two magic words having been spoken ("I do") do not improve the chances of a successful marriage.

Ron and Kimberly were married for six years, a second marriage for both. Each carried their own set of "baggage" from prior marriages. Perhaps, because their prior marriages had failed, Ron and Kimberly maintained a separate air about themselves, despite their being wed. They kept bank accounts separately, they kept their respective homes from these prior marriages, each had cars in their own name, and neither commingled any assets. Indeed, after two years of marriage to each other, they were still two single persons, happening to live under the same roof.

Neither of them actually needed the other person's money. In fact, both were separately employed and made respectable incomes as professionals. So, for all intents and purposes, these were two "single" people living together as a married couple. One day, Ron decided that the marriage was over.

"I'm getting a divorce," he matter-of-factly told his attorney. "The marriage is over. We both know that. How quickly can we get this mess straightened out?"

Indeed, there was very little "mess" to straighten out. There was no property acquired during the marriage. No children were born of the union and Kimberly was not pregnant. Since both parties were professionals with substantial incomes, the question of alimony was almost out of the question.

Ron thought this marital "mess" could probably be straightened out within weeks. The divorce complaint was filed and Ron promised his attorney that his wife would acknowledge service of process.

Two days later, Ron came back to his lawyer and proudly announced that everything was done and the "final papers" could be prepared.

"What do you mean 'Everything is done?'" Ron's attorney asked.

"I moved out of the house this morning," Ron proudly proclaimed, "took my furniture with me, and left the divorce complaint on the kitchen table," Ron announced.

No doubt, Ron unilaterally made up his own property settlement. He had divided up the assets, such as they were, by taking all of the property that he had acquired before the marriage, leaving behind all of the property that Kimberly had brought into the marriage at the marital home. Ron decided that Kimberly would stay in the rented home (of course, without speaking to her about this). He simply moved out one morning after she left for work. However, Ron "forgot" to tell Kimberly he was moving.

You could imagine Kimberly's rage when she returned home from work that evening only to find half of the house cleaned out and a divorce complaint left lying about the kitchen table. Ron was kind enough to leave a note which read, "Call me when you get home from work tonight." Hell hath no fury like a woman scorned.

While Ron might have imagined that there were no divorce issues to be litigated, Kimberly converted her anger into action. She was so surprised by her husband's emergency evacuation that she dug in her heels. In her answer to the complaint, she formally demanded alimony and scheduled a court hearing for Ron to maintain the *status quo* on all household payments pending the divorce.

The emergency court hearing was scheduled within a week. Kimberly appeared with her attorney who communicated her outrage at Ron's abandonment of his wife without one word of warning. Though it was seemingly irrelevant to the issue of divorce, Kimberly's attorney spared no detail as he explained to the divorce judge:

> *Your Honor, this supposedly good husband, Ron, slith-ered away from the rented marital home like a snake. . . but only after Kimberly had dutifully depart-ed for work. This cowardly man hid in the bushes until Kimberly had gone, knowing that she would be gone the entire day.*
>
> *As her modest car slipped from view, Ron summoned his SWAT Team of movers on his car telephone. Their moving van was fully staffed by a rough-necks who moved out half of the contents of this marital home in less than 90 minutes.*
>
> *Before Kimberly's morning coffee break had occurred, the moving van had closed its doors and rumbled away, leaving a whirlwind of dust in its wake as it*

bumped down the street, out of the subdivision, and to some secret, new household where Ron would hide away. At least, he left the cats. No doubt, they were not welcomed by his new landlord!

Of course, all of this was irrelevant, immaterial, and unrelated to the divorce. Nonetheless, Kimberly's attorney engendered the court's outrage at this rough departure with no word of warning. Struggling for a punishment to fit the crime, the judge ordered that Ron maintain the *status quo* during the divorce: Ron was to pay the rent on the marital home, the utilities and telephone bills, and was to rent replacement furniture for what he had taken (even though it was his own furniture) until the matter was finally resolved.

The judge also calculated that Ron's income was $10,000 higher than Kimberly's on an annual basis. Splitting the difference, the court ordered Ron to pay $100 alimony per week during the divorce. There was hardly a basis for alimony and less foundation for Ron to maintain the *status quo* given each party's substantial incomes. But that didn't stop the court from being outraged at Ron's unannounced departure, littering his trail with the divorce complaint. Just because Ron thought the marriage was over for him didn't mean it was over for Kimberly. The marriage is not over until the judge says it's over, regardless of when "the fat lady sings."

Ron was now in a real predicament. Because Kimberly opposed the divorce, the case might languish on the court's docket for as long as two years or more. Merely because Kimberly answered the complaint by saying that the marriage had not broken down to the extent that the objects of matrimony have been destroyed and there was some reasonable likelihood that the marriage could be preserved — Kimberly was entitled to a full-fledged divorce trial.

Kimberly would get a trial on whether or not the marriage had broken down, even though a marriage is broken down when one party says it is broken down. Meanwhile, alimony and *status quo* payments would continue. Ron could only hear the faint echo of a cash register in his mind.

Ron had two choices: appeal the judge's ruling (on alimony and *status quo* payments) or settle the divorce. An appeal might have been the righteous thing to do, however, appeals cost money. Ron's attorney quoted him a price of $3,500 to handle an interlocutory appeal of the judge's ruling. For that same $3,500, Ron could probably settle the case with Kimberly. That, of course, was the road taken. Ron settled the divorce by paying Kimberly $3,500, the divorce judgment was entered, and alimony payments ended.

Moral of the Story
Remember to say, "Goodbye." Don't simply walk out on a marriage, brief though it may have been. Don't unilaterally impose your own property settlement. You may outrage the judge who can design a "punishment to fit the crime."

Taking the Castle by Storm

Just because a divorce is filed does not mean that one person immediately has to move out of the house. A marital home owned by both parties is joint property, at least until the divorce judgment is granted. With children and a contested divorce, a judgment could take years. Meanwhile, everyone lives together — unless one spouse chooses to move out.

Fran wanted her soon-to-be ex-husband out of the house immediately. She complained about physical abuse in the past and was worried that, once she filed for divorce, he would become violent and she would become the victim. It is nearly impossible to evict a spouse upon filing of a divorce. Nonetheless, the attempt was made here.

Fran was sent to her doctor and the hospital to gather medical reports from those times when her husband had become violent and injured her. Fran also visited the police station to collect reports she had made over the previous months complaining about her husband's domestic violence. Though he had never been arrested for domestic violence, and Fran had never sought an injunction against his violence, she had been diligent in making police reports.

Upon filing the complaint, Fran signed an affidavit which itemized the dates, times, places, and witnesses to previous domestic violence. Copies of the hospital reports and police reports were attached. Fran also attached affidavits from witnesses who knew both parties and also believed that when Fran filed for divorce, her husband would become violent again.

When the divorce complaint was filed, Fran's attorney asked the court for an *ex parte* hearing without her husband's presence. Fran's attorney presented witnesses who testified to the husband's previous violence. The judge was impressed with the evidence and issued a temporary restraining order (TRO).

This TRO was an injunction stopping Fran's husband from remaining in the marital home until a hearing could be held on a preliminary injunction with all parties present. At such hearing, the court would decide whether or not to convert that TRO into a preliminary injunction, keeping the husband out of the house while the divorce was pending. A date was set for a full hearing and, meanwhile, the court issued an order expelling the husband from the house.

Fran's attorney had included an important paragraph in the TRO: the local police (where the marital home was located) were ordered by the judge to assist Fran in serving the court's order on her husband to assure there was no domestic violence. The process server was given the TRO and headed straight for the local police station.

Before the police accompanied the process server to deliver these divorce papers to Fran's husband, they checked the computer to see if the husband had any outstanding arrest warrants. Lo and behold, he had an outstanding out-of-state misdemeanor warrant. More than that, the police computer disclosed that Fran's husband had been imprisoned years ago for killing a police officer. Knowing that, no one was taking any chances.

The process server accompanied the officers to Fran's home. Six officers went to the house. When they arrived, they unracked and loaded their shotguns, ready for bear.

Fran's husband was taking a nap when his "guests" arrived. The process server quietly unlocked the front and back doors for the officers (having been given a key by Fran). The police officers stormed the castle from all entrances with their shotguns pointed. Fran's husband was rudely awakened. The officers arrested him on the outstanding warrant and escorted him from the marital home. On his way out the door, the process server politely handed him the divorce summons and complaint.

Fran was playing for keeps. Her husband never returned home again.

The Hostile Takeover

In the wild kingdom of corporate finance, consolidation, mergers, and acquisitions there can be weapons in the arsenal of the hostile takeover. But the hostile takeover is not limited to the wiles of corporate finance, it also roams freely among the soon-to-be-divorced.

Gloria did not look shrewd. Her rather pedestrian appearance was quite deceptive and men routinely underestimated her business acumen.

Gloria kept the accounts of a firm that served construction contractors. These contractors would frequently visit the business where Gloria worked. Newly divorced herself, Gloria exuded personality and charm.

Pete was a single father, separated from his first wife for many years. Working a sixty hour week to keep his business going, Pete rarely had the opportunity to socialize. Indeed, the occasional encounter with Gloria during the business day was a welcome refresher from Pete's grueling schedule.

A fairy tale was in the making. Princess Gloria and Peter the Great were soon married. Each, of course, had their own dower which they brought to the marriage. Gloria's dower consisted of a home she acquired during her previous marriage. More than that, Gloria protested, she had nothing but the blouse on her back.

Pete however, a custodial parent for many years and a successful entrepreneur, had acquired some wealth. His frugal lifestyle and modest dress concealed substantial liquid capital, a good home, solid investments, and a thriving contracting trade business. All of this, from Gloria's vantage point, made Pete a pretty good economic "catch."

Everything was a garden of roses for the first six years. Pete had sold his house and Gloria did the same. With the proceeds, they invested in a new nest. However, because Pete's former home was worth substantially more than Gloria's abode, he contributed approximately 75% of the investment capital for the new home. Gloria's 25% provided the balance of the down payment.

Pete and his son occupied the new marital home with Gloria and her son. Regrettably, the two boys never quite "hit it off." In fact, the friction between the two of them was tense daily fare. This strained the marriage and soon this became a house divided against itself.

Pete insisted on some discipline and contribution to the common welfare of the household while Gloria's son preferred the life of leisure that his mother's new spouse had brought to his formerly meager existence. This friction had become the wedge dividing the household. The children ultimately brought the marriage to the breaking point.

Rather than addressing these two young men, everyone denied out loud that there was a problem despite the daily wrestling match to make the household workable. In time, there was a breakdown in the marriage relationship and the objects of matrimony were destroyed; try hard as they may, there was no reasonable likelihood that the marriage could be preserved.

Gloria filed for divorce. Before doing so, she raided the joint bank account and withdrew a substantial amount of cash which constituted her "war chest" of legal fees. Indeed, her legal retainer was large enough to finance a brutal battle over the remaining assets.

Gloria displayed the "mining principal of divorce": what's mine is mine, and what's yours is mine. You may recall that Gloria purportedly had invested her life's savings (the proceeds from her former home) into the place she and Pete had purchased. What Pete didn't know, however, was that Gloria had been saving her weekly paycheck which had become a substantial "nest egg" after the six year marriage. Pete had never really needed Gloria's weekly pay check; he assumed she had used the money for their household expenses and her teenage son. However, Gloria had been saving her pay check, hiding it from Pete all the while. Indeed, love is blind.

Gloria's weekly pay check was cashed and then Gloria secretly deposited it into an out of town, small bank where Pete would never suspect to look. By being frugal with the family finances during this six year marriage, Gloria was able to make Pete's money last for everyone. Pete never suspected that Gloria could stretch a dollar so far, but she was quite ingenious and good at this. The frugal lifestyle everyone enjoyed was no different than what Pete had been used to during his many years as a single father.

Gloria insisted, in her divorce complaint, that she be awarded half of the marital home (though she contributed only 25% to its purchase price), half of a palatial summer cottage that Pete had constructed before their marriage, half of his business that had burgeoned over the last two decades, half of his pension, and half of everything else she could lay her hands on. Pete was at his wits' end because now, despite this relatively short term marriage, he might have to split all of his assets.

During the course of the divorce, Gloria insisted that she owned nothing. Interrogatories (written questions exchanged between the divorcing parties) disclosed nothing. When her deposition (sworn testimony before a court reporter) was taken, Gloria swore that she had no assets other than what she and Pete owned together. However, as the divorce progressed, it appeared that Gloria might have a "nest egg" buried somewhere. Pete decided to dig a little.

During the divorce, Gloria continued her job as an accountant. One pay day, Pete followed Gloria during her lunch period. Gloria first went to the local bank, where she and Pete had been doing business for years, cashed her check, and drove off in her car. Rather than returning to work, however, Gloria took a detour. After 30 minutes, she made one stop at a tiny bank, in a tiny town, with a tiny main office, and no branches. This was a financial institution that was so small you might have gone to a piggy bank first — unless you were Gloria!

Pete thought that this might not be the only place where Gloria was secreting assets. Through his attorney and at some expense, subpoenas were issued to dozens of financial institutions in the small surrounding towns within 30 minutes of where Gloria worked. When the subpoenas were answered and documents produced, the bountiful results came pouring in.

Not only did Gloria have a substantial amount of cash in that one small bank she visited during lunch, but she also had a $70,000 trust fund at another bank. At a different financial institution there was a safe deposit box. At a savings and loan, Gloria had certificates of deposit; she deposited the interest payments automatically into her mother's savings account.

When Pete concluded his investigation, Gloria was found to have more than $100,000 saved up during the marriage. Every pay check had been saved, plus this mysterious $70,000 trust fund was discovered. Gloria did not know the subpoenas were issued; she didn't understand that Pete had uncovered her nest eggs.

The interest income that Gloria was earning was being reported to the IRS under her mother's social security number. The only way to catch Gloria was to go on a "fishing expedition," spreading subpoenas all over town or among the relatives (including mothers-in-law).

At the divorce trial, Gloria was asked what assets she owned — other than joint marital assets with Pete. She denied any other assets. She repeated her denials. And upon being asked thrice, she swore to her previous lies.

Her shock was a sight to behold when she was confronted with myriad certificates of deposit, savings accounts, and trust funds. For the first time in years, she was speechless. She had no defense. The court concluded that Gloria had adequate assets. Moreover, her lies and deceit were some evidence that she had contributed to the marriage breakdown.

Some degree of fault was attributed to Gloria and the judge was persuaded that she should leave the marriage with exactly what she brought in: 25% of the value of the marital home and that was that. Gloria kept what she had hidden away while Pete kept everything else. Gloria's application of the "mining principle of divorce" produced only "fool's gold."

Moral of the Story

Know where the cash is going. Be sensitive to how much money is being spent on what. Watch the mail for indications of accounts at other financial institutions.

Evicting the Relatives

In second marriages, there can be a problem with your spouse's relatives — whether it's your in-laws or your step-children — living in the same house. When a divorce is filed, this increases tensions. But do you have to put up with the relatives staying at your house?

As the sole, titled owner to the house, you have some rights. You have the right to control who remains in that dwelling. If you don't like your in-laws staying for a week, a month, or forever, you might evict them by asking them to leave. The same may hold true for your adult step-children. If those step-children are no longer minors, and are otherwise healthy and capable of being on their own, you may evict them. If these relatives do not leave voluntarily, you may have to seek help from a landlord-tenant court.

•••••••••••••••••••••••••••••••••

Jack and Alice had lived together for several years. It was a second marriage for each. Both of them brought along their adult step-children to live with them in this new-found marital bliss. The bliss was short-lived, but the relatives stayed much longer.

Step-child Eric was a terror, except when he was sullen and depressed. When he wasn't either of these, he monopolized the telephone and otherwise disrupted Jack's home-based business.

After the divorce was filed, Eric would answer the telephone and tell Jack's potential clients that Jack no longer lived there, that he had closed his business, or that he had moved to South America. In time, Jack's income began to suffer.

Step-child Eric suffered from a terminal case of adolescence. This was particularly true before the divorce was filed and worsened thereafter. When he ate, he made a mess. When he brought his friends over, there were more of them, they were noisier, and stayed longer. Things deteriorated until one day Jack came home from work earlier than expected.

When Jack arrived home, he surprised Eric who was practicing some new-found telephone skills. Eric was tapping in to Jack's business telephone line. No doubt, Eric wanted free-and-unlimited long-distance telephone calls. He hoped to punish his step-father with the phone bill, except Jack nabbed him in the act.

When Jack came around the back of the house, he saw Eric attempting to tap into the telephone line. Jack approached silently, like a stealth bomber. But when Eric was surprised at being apprehended, the young boy struck out at Jack and slugged him. Jack didn't hesitate to reply in kind and gave one crashing blow to the young man who fell toward the ground and injured his elbow. The young boy was stunned, immediately screaming, "Uncle!"

The altercation ended, the lad leapt to his feet and sought asylum inside the house. Nursing his wounds, the boy needed more than a band-aid. The step-son got in his car, drove himself to the hospital, and returned hours later with his arm in a sling. Before returning home, however, Eric had stopped at the local police station to file criminal charges against his step-father for assault and battery.

When the police officers came to arrest Jack (for allegedly assaulting his step-son), there was a totally different story than the version which Eric had peddled at the police station. Nonetheless, the police arrested Jack for the "crime" charged.

Before the judge, Jack pled self-defense in retaliating to the first blow that had been thrown by Eric. The prosecutor refused to bargain the charges away or dismiss the complaint. The matter was tried before a judge who issued a *Not Guilty* ruling after a brief trial.

That was the last straw. Jack had enough. By a motion to the divorce judge (a court different than where the criminal charges were tried), Jack requested that Eric the Terrible be evicted from the home. The divorce judge complained that she had no jurisdiction over land-lord-tenant matters. She referred the divorcing parties back to the same judge who had heard the criminal matter; that court also handled eviction matters.

A landlord-tenant eviction was filed after the step-son was given his Notice to Quit. After refusing to vacate the premises, legal action was taken to formally evict him from the marital home.

The eviction matter was tried before the same judge who found Jack not guilty on the assault and battery charges. The court determined that because the step-mother's name also was on the title to the marital home, she had just as much right to allow Eric (her own son) to reside in the home as Jack had the right to allow his own son to reside there. The judge refused to evict Eric. However, the judge warned that any further misbehavior on Eric's part would cause the judge to evict him as a nuisance.

The warning was ineffective for Eric. He and his mother both continued a pattern and practice of mischief and malicious tricks. Finally, the divorce judge evicted both of them from the marital home, even before the divorce was concluded.

Moral of the Story
If you can't evict unwanted relatives through the divorce court, you might try the landlord-tenant court. If that doesn't work, go back to divorce court and try again.

You Can't Go Home Again

Possession may be nine-tenths of the law. When it comes to

the marital home, whoever surrenders possession temporarily may surrender the marital home permanently.

Nancy and Don had a fine lakefront home. Both were hoping to keep the home after the divorce. By the end of the divorce, it was unclear whether either of them would get the house. The divorce had dragged on for more than three years. Neither could afford to live alone. It was such a beautiful home that both continued to live together even after the divorce judgment. Technically, the divorce judgment required that the marital home be sold, though no listing agreement had been signed.

As months passed after the divorce, Don began pursuing another woman, though still living with his ex-wife in the "marital" home. One wintery weekend, Don and his friends went up north for a snowmobiling safari. As the sun set and dusk fell, it became impossible to see what lie ahead. Oblivious to the shifting shadows, Don's snowmobile careened forward. Tragedy was just around the corner. Don's snowmobile crashed into a ravine, tossing him against a tree, and injuring him severely.

After Don arrived at the hospital, the doctor plastered casts on broken bones, taped broken ribs, and wrapped an injured skull. While ambulatory, Don limped around on crutches, though otherwise unable to take care of himself. Being several hundred miles away from home, and unable to drive himself back while his "friends" continued to enjoy the rest of their snowmobile vacation, Don decided to telephone his new girlfriend — to see if she would fetch him from the north woods.

This new woman came to the rescue, driving hundreds of miles on a cold dark night to a tiny hospital in a small town. She picked Don up from the lobby and drove him back to the city where he lived. He was obviously unable to care for himself. Needing a place to stay, the now-divorced Don could not very well return to the lakefront home where he and his ex-wife resided. Don could hardly ask his divorced wife to wait on him, hand and foot. Being a Good Samaritan, Don's lady friend invited him to stay for the night, for the week, for the month. He did.

In due course, the broken bones mended, the wounds healed, and the torn muscles began to work again like normal. After a while, Don was recovering well and took leave of his new lady friend. Packing himself into the car, he went "back home."

Having been divorced, Don had excused himself from the common courtesy of advising his wife-turned-roommate of his whereabouts. When Don never returned home from his snowmobiling weekend, divorced or not, Nancy was worried to death about him.

Finally suspecting some new romance, but not knowing for sure, Nancy had called Don's snowmobiling friends for some word. They told of the snowmobile accident, the hospitalization, and Don's discharge into the arms of *the other woman.* Nancy was furious, not because of her ex-husband's post-divorce infidelity, but because of his insensitivity, lack of courtesy, and — let us be frank — rudeness in failing to advise his *ex-* why he never returned home from the snowmobiling sojourn.

During the several weeks after the snowmobile accident, Nancy began to resolve her anger. She had concluded that Don had moved out. She rearranged the furniture. Packed his clothes in boxes, taped them shut, marked them, and stored them in the garage. She took down those ugly paintings (that Don had wanted so badly in the divorce settlement). Nancy sent all of Don's things packing.

When Don decided he had healed and would return home, he showed up at the door. To his surprise, the locks had been changed. No doubt, his name was still on the home's title; Don still owned the marital home jointly with his *ex-.* However, regardless of whose name appeared on the paperwork, he was locked out.

Don was livid. He immediately stormed (or, rather, limped) to his attorney's office. Outraged, Don insisted that his attorney immediately bring a motion for his readmission to the "marital home" until sold, as the divorce decree had allowed. The divorce judge, a conservative family man, didn't exactly see it Don's way.

Don was a caricature of himself as he was raised up on two crutches before the judge's bench. The judge, himself a behemoth of some measurable size, peered gravely over his reading spectacles, conducting the questioning:

Q.   *You have a girlfriend?*

A.   *Well, yes Judge, ever since the divorce was granted.*

Q.   *No wonder your marriage got wrecked.*

A.   *But, your Honor, you granted us a divorce nearly two months ago and. . . .*

Q.   *I don't care what I granted you. If I didn't say you could live in that house after the divorce, then you can't live there. You never asked me if you could stay there. I am the one who's in charge here. You're out of that house, now, Buster.*

A.   *But. . . but. . . but . . . .*

Don's attorney pleaded desperately for his client's right, if only to stay in the home until sold. The plea not only fell on deaf ears, but raised the judge's ire. "Can't my client at least go home and pick up his clothes?" Don's attorney interceded.

"He has until five o'clock tonight to get all of his belongings out of the house. Crippled or not, on crutches or on a skateboard, with or without broken ribs!"

Done with his tirade, the judge then smiled most pleasantly bidding Don, "Good-bye and good luck." The Bailiff called the next case."

Moral of the Story
Possession is 9/10ths of the law. Surrender possession temporarily and you may sacrifice your rights permanently. Remember, once you leave, you can't go home again.

Look a Gift Horse in the Mouth

One complication about divorce that is boring but crucial is tax law. The rule is: whoever takes a marital asset through a divorce judgment also takes the basis of that asset. If the basis of a home (the original purchase price, considering certain adjustments) is $100,000, the spouse who is awarded that marital home in a divorce proceeding, also takes the $100,000 basis.

If 10 years after the divorce, the spouse who received the home sells it for $300,000, realizing a capital gain, there can be tax consequences, unless the proceeds are reinvested in another home. If there are tax consequences when an asset is received in a divorce, you need to be aware of the financial repercussions.

Remember that whoever takes the marital home, or any other real property, should calculate the net value. A $100,000 home is not a $100,000 value to the recipient. Deduct sales commissions (7% to 10%); costs of sale (1%); capital gains tax (zero to 31%); and miscellaneous closing costs (1% to 3%). After deductions, a $100,000 parcel may only net $50,000 or so. Consider net values, not gross values.

Keeping the House Forever

The most valued asset over which divorcing parties squabble is the marital home. The judicial *rule of thumb* is the parties agree what should be done with the marital home; if there is disagreement, the court can order the marital home sold, the mortgages and other encumbrances paid off, and the net proceeds divided. Where the parties cannot agree as to value and possession, the home can be sold. Short of selling the home, which is rare, there are options.

One party usually expresses a preference to keep the house. Ironically, the party who desires to keep the residence often has the poorest cash flow or earning capacity. Comparable housing (assuming some equity in the property) should be hard to find at a lower rental rate.

The party retaining possession of the dwelling can give a mortgage for half of the value of the home to the other party . The mortgage normally bears interest, ranging from nominal interest (7%) to more competitive interest (the prevailing 30-year mortgage rate when the divorce is granted). Interest and terms are negotiated.

Retaining the residence often comes with certain restrictions. Customarily, a spouse continues to reside in the residence provided that the children are under the age of 18, have not yet graduated from high school, the recipient spouse remains living, and no unrelated member of the opposite sex moves into the martial home.

As long as a mortgage encumbers the home, both of the mortgagors (the husband and the wife) remain equally obligated on the mortgage until paid in full. When the house is sold, there must be enough equity to pay off the mortgage. Otherwise, both mortgagors remain equally liable to the mortgagee on any deficiency — regardless of what the divorce judgment says.

Merely because a divorce judge gives possession to one party, that does not forgive the other party from being liable on the mortgage. A judge cannot undue a contractual relationship between a mortgagor and a mortgagee by granting a divorce to one of the mortgagors. Simply put, there are no magic words that can be recited in a divorce judgment that will "hold harmless" the spouse who is denied possession of the family abode. You remain liable on the mortgage. . . regardless of what the judge says and regardless of the language that you put in the judgment of divorce.

The only way to free yourself of the mortgage obligation is to get a release from the mortgagee (bank, mortgage company, or the like). If the mortgagee says that one mortgagor is no longer responsible for the mortgage, and that pledge is put in writing, signed by all parties affected, then the obligation is released. Absent such a release by all mortgagees, a divorce judge can say or do nothing that will forgive a mortgage.

Before allowing your spouse to have possession of the marital home, if you remain obligated on the mortgage, be confident that there is enough equity in the home to pay off such mortgage. If the equity is insubstantial, then do not agree to be co-obligated on the mortgage; condition awarding the house to your spouse on the grant of a brand new mortgage for which you are not obligated in the least.

●●●●●●●●●●●●●●●●●●●●●●●●●●●●●●●●

Alicia and Frank continued to live together after their divorce had been filed. They had purchased a home years earlier. When Frank filed for divorce, Alicia decided that she wanted the house. . . forever.

Frank would not voluntarily leave the marital home after the divorce was filed. He too wanted the house and was not about to surrender so easily. Alicia, fixed on her goal of keeping the house forever, designed a plan and set forth to implement it. There would be gorilla warfare, if necessary, and she would get the house.

During the divorce, the relationship between Frank and Alicia was strained. There was little communication. However, Alicia's strategy was to make life as miserable as possible for her soon-to-be *ex-*. Alicia did some of the things that you expect any determined individual to do under the circumstances: she stopped doing Frank's laundry, she stopped cooking his meals, and she stopped picking up after him. Together they lived separate lives under the same roof.

As this was a small, three bedroom house, and the children occupied two bedrooms, Alicia decided it was wholly inappropriate for Frank to continue sharing *her* bed. Before the divorce, it had been *their* bed. In short order, she stuffed all of Frank's belongings into boxes and exiled him to the family room. She had a dead bold lock installed on what once was *their* bedroom door. When Frank came home late that night, he was denied admission to the sacred chamber. He found the pillow and blankets that Alicia had set out for him in the family room and took up residence there.

Alicia knew Frank's weaknesses better than he did. She knew, for example, that Frank loathed her family. Accordingly, Alicia proceeded to invite a different group of relatives over each weekend. Blood being thicker than water, some of Alicia's relatives joined merrily in her strategy of harassment and adverse possession of the home. This bothered Frank tremendously and, soon, he would leave on Friday mornings, not returning until the next Monday evening — leaving Alicia and the weekends to her relatives.

It was becoming clear to Frank that there was "no place like home." Frank soon took up a room at the local YMCA.

The divorce was not a quick affair. Indeed, Alicia obstinately refused to agree on marital assets. Accordingly, the divorce dragged on for nearly three years. All the while, Frank endured his monastic residence at the "Y."

When the divorce trial finally came, Alicia presented her evidence to the judge. She demonstrated that Frank had not lived in the marital house for nearly three years and could afford to live elsewhere. The children were enrolled in local schools and it would be disruptive for them to move. Frank was quite capable of maintaining a separate residence (such as it was) on his earnings.

Alicia argued that she and Frank should divide the value of the marital home. Alicia would give Frank a mortgage at 7% interest for one half of the net value of the residence. The judge ordered that Frank quit claim his interest in the house to Alicia, that he be granted the legal position of a mortgagee. Frank was allowed to record his mortgage. Alicia's strategy had worked and she kept the house forever.

Moral of the Story

If you wish to keep the house, keep the house and do not surrender possession even temporarily. If you surrender the marital home during the divorce, then you might sacrifice the home forever. Considering your sanity, however, a small apartment is an improvement over a psychiatric floor.

Surprise Honey, We're Moving

The heaviest albatross to carry through a divorce is the unresolved possession of the marital home. Even when the home inevitably must be sold, one party often has the incentive to protract the divorce to remain in the marital home as long as possible. This is common.

If neither spouse can afford to keep up the house, then the home must be sold at the end of the divorce. However, for as long as the divorce carries on, both parties are equally entitled to stay in the residence. Usually the primary wage earner (if there is one) will be required to maintain the *status quo* of household payments (utilities, mortgage, insurance, taxes, etc). Because a divorce unilaterally cannot be granted by a judge without a trial unless the parties agree on how to divide assets, the occupancy of the house continues to be joint until a final judgment is granted.

Often, the sale of the marital home can bring a divorce to a close. If a judge can be persuaded that neither party has the resources alone to pay for upkeep and expenses of the marital home, then the home can be listed for sale by order of the court. If either party refuses to cooperate in the listing or sale of the home, then the court can appoint a receiver to take charge of selling the home. The trick is to sell the property before the divorce is filed so that this major asset will not drag people down like an anchor in the mud.

●●●●●●●●●●●●●●●●●●●●●●●●●●●●●●●●

Alan and Lori had a marital home, plus a couple of children. Alan's assessment of the situation was this: when he filed for divorce, Lori would argue that she should be awarded the home with the children and Alan should pay the mortgage in lieu of alimony until the children were all age 18. Alan would never see the equity that he had invested in the house until after his youngest child graduated from high school. Alan's strategy was to sell the property *before* Lori knew that he contemplated divorce.

The marriage of Alan and Lori was certainly in rough straights and on the rocks. Alan was less than candid when he suggested to Lori that they try to "work things out." In fact, Alan had a "solution" in mind: he suggested the "geographic cure."

They would sell the house and move to a new city. Alan could get a new job, the kids could find a new school, Lori could develop new friends, and everyone could *start all over again*. Because the marriage was important to Lori, she enlisted in Alan's geographic cure.

Together they listed the house for sale and agreed upon a price. The house was sold and after the closing, there was a fine chunk of money deposited in the bank, ready for Alan and Lori to begin a new day.

With the closing behind them, Alan and Lori packed their belongings to move. Their plan pleased Lori because Alan readily agreed to move to the town where Lori's sisters and brothers lived. Luckily, Alan had found work in a city near there. Lori found this a good sign, it made her hopeful that the marriage would be preserved.

Everything was packed in the U-Haul truck. Alan had arranged for Lori and the children to fly ahead while he drove the rental truck. He saw Lori and the children off at the airport. They planned to take up temporary residence at the home of Lori's sister. Alan was scheduled to drive there over several days.

Alan did drive the moving truck, but not to the city where Lori had taken the children. Rather, he stopped to unload in the nearby town where he had located his new job. Alan stopped the truck at the apartment where he had made arrangements for a separate place for him to stay. Alan unloaded all the boxes that contained his belongings and left the rest of the personalty in the truck. Before leaving town, Alan had gone to the bank, taking two cashier's checks, each for exactly one-half of the proceeds from the sale of the home.

After setting himself up in his new apartment, Alan drove the moving truck to Lori's sister's place. Alan gave her the check for one-half of the proceeds. Lori was one very unhappy lady, left with two children and a moving van full of boxes she never had expected to unpack alone. She deposited her check and started over again.

Moral of the Story
If you get rid of the house, you get rid of some "heavy baggage" which may bring a divorce to a grinding halt. Also, keep your ear to the rail if your spouse says, "Surprise, Honey, we're moving."

154

chapter 9 PERSONAL PROPERTY

Pet Divorce Issues

Both dog lovers and cat lovers get divorced. In the process, somebody ends up with custody. . . of the pets.

Pets are personal property. Regardless of who the owner is, which spouse raised the animal, the pet is a marital asset. The divorce judge has jurisdiction to divide the pets — hopefully with some wisdom other than that of Solomon.

Imagine the following terrible situation. Joan comes into a wonderful marriage and brings two beautiful abyssinian cats. Harold is a dastardly fellow and after filing for divorce, gathers up all of the venom that he can muster and decides that Joan's cats will be his cats. Perhaps, even as he leaves the marital home with wardrobe and records in hand, he packs the kitty litter and the cats as well. It will be up to the divorce judge to seek some justice in the face of such feline thievery.

Walkin' the Dog

Jim was happily married for many years to Rosanne. Jim was a surgeon and had few hobbies outside of his marriage other than hunting. Rex was his own hunting dog. While Jim was performing surgery and caring for patients, his good wife Rosanne would spend hours caring for Rex; she groomed him, took him to the veterinarian, walked him, fed him, and played with him at the park. Indeed, other than the few hunting trips each year that Rex took with his "owner," the dog Rex had imprinted on Rosanne as his "real mother."

As the divorce was filed, the parties discussed living apart. One of them had to move. Jim found a place to live, but it was too tiny for Rex, the great dog, who would have no backyard for romping around.

Dr. Jim brought a motion for temporary custody. . . of Rex. The judge wrestled with the issue, dog-eared as it may have been. The court determined this custody battle by allowing Rosanne to keep the family dog and gave Jim visitation on alternate weekends from Friday at 6:00 p.m. until Sunday at noon. Because they had "joint custody" of Rex, both parties were required to share veterinarian expenses, periodontal bills, the costs of food (which for Rex was no mean fare), and other reasonable and necessary expenses. But that didn't solve the problem.

When hunting season came, Rosanne (retaining one last issue that she could use to exercise control over Dr. Jim) told her ex-husband that hunting season did not fall within his weekend for visitation. It took Dr. Jim one more motion to get the court to award specific visitation during hunting week. Now, annually and religiously, Rex and Jim go off for their scheduled hunts, only to leave Rex's "wicked stepmother" behind.

•••••••••••••••••••••••••••••••

Sometimes, the threat of malice is deceptively employed. Doug and Chelsea had a fine black Labrador Retriever named Sue. Sue loved to hunt and was "Doug's dog." When Chelsea and her husband broke up, Chelsea packed her bags and moved hundreds of miles away, taking Sue in the back of her car and depriving Doug of his first love — the dog!

Divorce negotiations ensued, property was distributed, the silverware divided, and all issues were resolved except for one last issue — that dog named Sue. When Doug insisted that, as a nonnegotiable, final condition of resolving the divorce, he must regain custody of his fine black Labrador Retriever Sue, Chelsea refused. She protested not that she didn't want to give the dog back to Doug, but that she *couldn't* return the Lab. But, why?

Chelsea tearfully explained that when she left town, the dog Sue was so heartbroken that she leapt out of the car at one of the expressway rest stops, bolted into the woods, heading vaguely back in the direction of the marital home that she had just left. It brought a tear to Doug's eye. The thought of Sue roaming around out there in the fields, or worse yet, near the expressways, without her master was something that made his stomach wretch.

Doug's sorrow converted to anger in a "New York minute." Not only did he want the dog back but, also, he wanted "war reparations." In the course of the ensuing negotiations to resolve this last issue, it began to be clear that the good dog Sue may not have run off *permanently*. In fact, it was hinted that maybe even Sue had returned.

The negotiations took a strange twist when Chelsea offered her soon-to-be ex-husband the opportunity to be reunited with his dog Sue — for a price! Just before the ransom that was being demanded by Chelsea began to creep toward extortion, negotiations were concluded.

In exchange for $4,000, the good dog Sue was joyfully reunited with her lost master. Apparently, Sue had run off at the rest stop, however, Chelsea omitted telling her husband that the dog was caught soon thereafter at a nearby farm house. Chelsea had told the truth — that is, the half-truth. Chelsea never really liked that dog anyway.

A Rabbit's Foot

Sometimes, malice laces divorce proceedings, weaving its way into the realm of family petdome.

Peter Rabbit was a lop-eared, English bunny. Fred purchased this little cottontail for his wife Martha as an Easter surprise one year. Martha never forgets the day when she came home from work to find Fred sitting on the couch, with his two hands cupped on his chest. Yet, from beneath the cup of Fred's hands peeked a glassy-eyed rabbit with ears as long as its body. Martha was delighted.

Regrettably, Martha's delight did not mirror her relationship with Fred during their short-termed marriage. Fred's malice took shape and, on his way out the door, when Martha sent him packing for his reckless expenditure of marital funds and other sins too numerous to mention, Fred absconded with Peter Rabbit.

Now when the judge was informed that Martha's "rabbit died," it had nothing to do with pregnancy. Fred meant that Peter Rabbit had met his Maker. The judge learned that Fred stopped by the local poultry shop on his way out of town and deposited Fred for someone's anonymous Sunday supper. Fred's malice stirred the Judge to place a "bounty" on Peter Rabbit's head.

After taking testimony, the judge assessed a value of the pet rabbit that was martyred by Fred: the pet rabbit was valued at $3,500, plus attorney fees, and plus costs of the valuation hearing. When it was all over, only Peter Rabbit was sorrier than Fred that the whole affair had happened.

One Way to Skin a Cat

Stanley and Barbara had recently divorced. It was one of those bitter separations. No one left smiling. After the divorce was granted, Stanley and his attorney went out to "celebrate." Normally, celebrating is not what you want to do after a divorce judgment has been entered. However, Stanley and his lawyer went out for drinks, nonetheless. A few drinks at a local bar turned into a binge. After becoming "well-lubricated," Stanley and his attorney decided there should be some retribution for Barbara to pay in this divorce.

Quite intoxicated, Stanley and his lawyer broke into Barbara's home. The attorney saw Max, Barbara's seven-month-old kitten. For "fun," they put Max into the microwave and turned it on. . . just for "a few seconds."

Max was alive when they scooped him out of the microwave. "We just put him on the floor and ran," Stanley confessed. The little kitten curled up and died.

That wasn't the end of the story for Stanley and his attorney. Both were found guilty of their criminal acts, sentenced to substantial probation and community service, and fined $1,000 each. That was only the beginning of problems, however, for Stanley's attorney. The cat's owner, Barbara, filed a complaint against the lawyer, asking that he be disbarred. It remains to be seen whether or not Stanley's lawyer will ever practice law again.

Moral of the Story
A divorce court is often willing to deal with the pet issue of custody. Pets can be considered marital property and a court may award custody of these family favorites in a divorce. However, if you care for the canine or feel for your feline, get the dog to the kennel and the kitty to the cattery *before* **the divorce papers start flying.**

Asset for Me, Liability for You

One spouse gets the asset and the other the liability. Claudia and John had been married for some years. They were a two car family; one was his and the other hers. John worked for an automobile manufacturer and purchased cars on the company plan. The money to purchase the cars was borrowed from the company's financial subsidiary where the husband worked.

The car which Claudia drove was in her name, even though the finance company had recorded a lien against the title of that car. The lien was to secure the money that John had borrowed to pay for Claudia's car. In the divorce, the motor vehicles were equally divided; John was granted his vehicle and Claudia granted hers. However, Claudia was required to hold John harmless and pay the underlying obligation for the motor vehicle herself.

There were no children of this marriage and Claudia was intent on starting a new life somewhere else, far away. After the divorce was granted, Claudia liquidated her assets, packed her bags, and hopped into the brand new car that her husband had purchased, financed by the husband's employer.

Claudia neglected an important business matter. When she moved, her automobile insurance lapsed and she was left with no coverage for theft or collision. The divorce judgment was silent about who was to insure the vehicle. While everyone assumed that Claudia was to maintain her own car insurance, that didn't happen. Halfway across the country, on her journey to a new life, Claudia was the unfortunate victim of a car theft. Her new vehicle was stolen, there was no insurance to cover the proceeds, and yet the debt remained due and payable. John, her new *ex-*, got stuck with the $10,000 car note.

Since Claudia liquidated all of the assets and disappeared to some new city, far away, John was left "holding the bag."

Moral of the Story
For every asset you give away, transfer all liabilities connected with that asset. Remember, any liability for which you remain obligated after the divorce places you at risk for tax consequences. Once you discharge that liability, you may have no

recourse against your spouse if the divorce judgment fails to protect you.

Injunction *Freeze Frame*

Meaningful protection is the *ex parte* mutual property injunction. This is an order of the court forbidding either party from removing, secreting, hiding, or otherwise disposing of any asset during the divorce. *Ex parte* property injunctions are liberally granted if mutual; however, the mutual *ex parte* property injunction stops both your spouse and you from disposing of marital assets.

If you intend to secure a mutual *ex parte* property injunction, then muster all the assets you need prior to the injunction being issued. For example, perhaps you may need a substantial retainer for your attorney; you may require a security deposit or prepaid rent for a new apartment; or you may want to pay off joint marital debts if your creditworthiness is at risk. Any of these things must be done before you file for divorce and before any mutual *ex parte* injunction is filed.

Sample Property Injunction

State of Michigan
[County] County Circuit Court

[Plaintiff],   Case No. *[Number]*
        Plaintiff
vs.   Hon. *[Judge]*
        Circuit Judge
[Defendant],
        Defendant

Ex Parte Mutual Property Injunction

At a session of said Court
held in the chambers of
the above-referenced Judge on

_____

Hon. *[Judge]*
Circuit Judge

On reading the verified Motion of *[Plaintiff]*, and it appearing that immediate and irreparable injury, loss and damage will result to the *[Plaintiff]* unless this *Ex Parte* Mutual Injunctive Order is issued without notice to *[Defendant]* and the Court being fully advised in the premises; it is. . .

Injunction

ORDERED that *[Plaintiff]* and *[Defendant]* (as well as any officers, agents, servants, employees, attorneys and those persons in active concert or participation with *[Defendant]* who receive actual notice of this Order by personal service or otherwise) DO ABSOLUTELY DESIST AND REFRAIN FROM:

(A)**Personal Assets**. Selling, assigning, concealing, mortgaging, encumbering, destroying, transferring, removing from the marital home (where applicable), placing them beyond the other party's reach, or otherwise disposing of the parties' personal assets, household furniture, appliance, clothing, personal effects, or other assets, except for necessities, of either or both of these parties;

(B)**Financial Assets**. Withdrawing, removing, releasing, closing, or otherwise disposing of any monies, bank accounts, certificates of deposit (CD), individual retirement accounts (IRA), or other evidence of deposit (including safe deposit boxes) at any financial institution (whether it be a bank, credit union, savings and loan association, stock brokerage, or otherwise)

(C)**Beneficiaries**. Changing the present beneficiaries of any trust, life or accident insurance policy, bank account, cash management fund, or tax exempt bond fund account of the parties.

Injunction Effective

ORDERED that this Injunction shall be valid when served upon the attorney for *[Plaintiff]* and *[Defendant]* (or their attorney) and remains in effect during this lawsuit (a) unless by mutual, written agreement of the parties, or (b) until further order of this Court; and, it is further. . .

Civil Contempt of Court

Ordered that failure to comply with this Injunction will subject the violator to civil contempt of court and an order will issue to show cause why this Court should not hold that violator in contempt of court for failure to comply.

Violation of this Injunction will not subject either party to criminal contempt of court [as provided in MCL 552.14(4)]; and, it is further. . .

No Bond Required

ORDERED that no bond is required because this is a divorce action.

Issued on the ____ day of _____, 199___ at _____ o'clock in the _____ noon and valid until further order of this Court.

_____
[Circuit Judge]

Risking Your Credit Rating

Divorce proceedings not only divide up the assets, but allocate liabilities. The transfer of every asset should include the liability associated with that asset. Thus, the spouse who takes the marital home, should also pay off all mortgages, liens, assessments, insurance premiums, and taxes associated with that marital home.

The same holds true for an automobile: whoever takes a particular motor vehicle must pay off all lienholders. Matters become more complex, however, when both parties remain liable for debts, and yet one party is awarded a specific asset with which a debt is associated.

When a loan is obtained, with rare exception, both husband and wife become obligated to pay off the balance. Let us assume that, in a divorce, a wife is awarded the sailboat and is required to pay the boat loan. But if the husband remains liable on that boat loan, a divorce court cannot excuse him.

Though the divorce judgment may require your spouse to hold you harmless from the underlying boat loan, you are not actually released from liability for that loan. You still remain liable to the loan company. . . regardless of what the divorce judgment says.

When the divorce judgment orders that your spouse will "hold you harmless," it does *not* mean that the loan company will hold you harmless. If your spouse defaults on the loan, you will still pay the balance due — it's just that your spouse may have to reimburse you. . . some day.

So, in our example, the wife is given the sailboat subject to the loan and a promise to hold the husband harmless from payments for that loan. Yet, there still could be a problem. Let us say that the wife defaults on the loan and the sailboat is repossessed and sold; however, the sale price fell short of the amount needed to pay off the loan and there is a deficiency. Who is going to pay the deficiency balance due for the sailboat loan? The answer, regardless of what the divorce judgment says, is *both parties* will pay. How do you protect yourself under these circumstances?

The protection is simple. If there is a balance due on a loan, the party who is awarded the asset must first pay the balance due. Otherwise, the asset is sold and the net proceeds are divided. To do otherwise, risks the credit worthiness of the spouse who remains obligated on the loan. To do anything less is risky business.

Sneaking Cookies from the Cookie Jar

Sneaking a few treats from the cookie jar ahead of time is one way to get your just desserts. However, you must help yourself to these goodies well before you file for divorce if you expect your spouse to pay half.

Need a new wardrobe? Perhaps a little shopping might be in order to outfit yourself in the style to which you would like to become accustomed. As long as you don't become lavishly exorbitant in your spending, you may be able to buy yourself "a few little things" before the divorce is filed.

Normally, a judge will divide the liabilities of a divorce in effect as of the date the parties stop cohabiting together as husband and wife. While this is not always true, it is the customary procedure.

If you need a new car, perhaps you can persuade your spouse to invest in one for you. . . provided your spouse does not anticipate the divorce is imminent.

How about finishing up that educational program you have let languish for much too long? This too should be completed before the divorce is filed. The financially shrewd spouse will view divorce as an event to be planned some months or years in advance, rather than a precipitous impulse reaction to some "straw that broke the camel's back."

If your spouse is getting prepared for some "big event," and you're not exactly sure what that event is (or even whether it includes you), then beware of the stock piling of assets and accruing liabilities. A pre-divorce spending spree is an event for which you may share half the cost — after the divorce is filed.

"Can I Sign Your Name, Honey?"

The second oldest trick in the book starts with the question, "Can I sign your name, Honey?" We assume you know the oldest trick.

To sign your spouse's name to legal documents (particularly negotiable instruments, such as checks and credit card charges slips) can be the basis for serious dispute in a later divorce.

Phyllis and Charles were married for a decade. During that time, Phyllis worked for a school system that had made generous contributions to her pension plan. Under this retirement plan, Phyllis was able to liquidate the entire pension upon retirement from active employment as a teacher.

After being married ten years to Charles, Phyllis quit her job as a teacher to go back to school to become an attorney; she cashed in her pension plan to live off the proceeds while attending law school.

Phyllis had advised Charles that she would be leaving him, filing for divorce, and moving out of state to attend law school. The two agreed on dividing their assets and had accomplished that quite amicably, even before the divorce papers were filed. Charles even offered to hire an attorney who would prepare the divorce papers for both of them. With an equal division of the assets and her cash in hand, Phyllis parted ways with Charles.

Phyllis had applied for a full payoff from her pension plan and had given the school retirement system her forwarding address. Charles had remained behind at the couple's apartment. Regrettably, there was some mix up with the pension board which mailed Phyllis's check to her old apartment where Charles still lived.

Charles received the pension check for tens of thousands of dollars and decided that it was a "marital asset," half of which he was entitled. This was a "simple divorce." Phyllis never spoke with the attorney whom Charles hired to prepare the papers. The divorce judgment was silent about the issue of pension and retirement plans.

Phyllis had made a serious mistake during the marriage. She had always turned her checks over the Charles and he had handled the finances. In fact, she never even signed her name to the back of her own checks but had allowed Charles to endorse these checks for her. Charles would deposit them into the common account, pay all the bills, and function as the comptroller of the marriage.

When Charles saw the substantial retirement check, he began to drool. Charles then did what he had always done with Phyllis's checks: he endorsed and deposited it into the joint account at the bank (which he had never closed), and then promptly withdrew one-half for himself. Because the divorce was done "on the cheap" by an attorney who failed to ask enough probing questions, the parties got what they paid for. To Phyllis, that was half of what she wanted; to Charles, that was twice as much as he deserved.

After some months, Phyllis was still missing her payment from the retirement system. She began to pester the pension board. Phyllis ultimately learned that her pension had been liquidated. Phyllis, having received no check, insisted on seeing a copy of the check that had been sent to her. Again, several months passed before the check copy was located. When Phyllis finally saw the check copy where her "signature" appeared, it was clear: Charles had cashed the check.

Phyllis then attempted to reach Charles but, regrettably, he had moved and had an unlisted telephone number. After some substantial effort, and a private detective, Phyllis finally located Charles and had a letter delivered to him. She threatened to sue him unless he turned over her pension monies.

Not wanting to be on the wrong end of a lawsuit, Charles quickly sent Phyllis a check, not for the entire amount of the pension, but only for one-half of the pension cash out. The entire mess ended back before divorce judge to determine who should get how much of the pension since the divorce judgment was silent in that regard.

The divorce judge took evidence and determined that half of the pension was earned by Phyllis before she had married Charles, while the other half was earned during the marriage to Charles. Because of that, only one-half of the pension was a marital asset.

Therefore, Charles was only entitled to 50% of one-half of the pension — or one-fourth of the pension. Charles had to distribute back to Phyllis the excess share that he had failed to give to her. It was a mess. It dragged out. Extra attorney fees and costs were incurred to do it right the second time.

Moral of the Story
It doesn't matter what you intend should happen, if it isn't in writing and part of the divorce judgment, then your intentions are shaped like the wind. Get a good divorce attorney, pay a reasonable fee, otherwise you will get what you pay for in the end — and that may be nothing. Don't let your spouse sign your name on checks, other negotiable instruments, or contracts which may oblige you to pay money to another; if you do, it is you who may pay in the end.

Mustering the Assets

Sometimes, the best advice about cash assets is to withdraw

all joint assets and take personal, sole, and exclusive possession of them — before you file for divorce. In any event, at least withdraw half.

Assets in joint accounts should be removed immediately before the divorce is filed and redeposited in a different financial institution in your own name. This prevents your spouse from going to the bank and "stealing the family jewels."

If there is real or personal property in your spouse's name alone, beware. Your spouse might have assets where your name does not appear on the legal title. A certificate of deposit in your spouse's name alone does not entitle you to cash the CD. Sometimes, married couples can own real property in their own separate name, even though their spouse might have (what is historically known as) a "dower interest" in such property.

There are different ways to protect property (real or personal) which is in the name of one spouse alone. Consider doing two things: first, get an *ex parte* property injunction; second, record a *lis pendens* against the title of any such property.

An *ex parte* property injunction is an order of the court. It is granted by a judge without any notice to your spouse. It enjoins or orders your spouse not to sell, dispose, secrete, conceal, or otherwise manipulate any assets, whether in joint names or held by one spouse alone.

To record a *lis pendens* against the title to property advises the world that there is a divorce proceeding and the divorce court may grant a judgment which could split up the title to this property. The filing of a *lis pendens* on a parcel of property is an extra precaution against the 1% chance your spouse would violate a court order and sell property despite issuance of a property injunction.

If there is personal property in the name of your spouse alone, serve a copy of the *ex parte* property injunction on the bank, brokerage house, insurance company, or other place from where assets can be withdrawn. Serve a copy of a property injunction (either by a process server or any other way allowed by your state's law) on a company which controls marital assets in your spouse's name alone; this adds an ounce of precaution (which is worth more than a pound of cure). Only in rare circumstances will someone violate a court order not to sell assets. But when it happens, the situation may be irreversible, or costly to cure.

Once the asset is spent, it's gone. A divorce judge can take the casual attitude that "it will all come out in the wash" at the end of the divorce. That may not do you any good now or then. Take the precaution of serving an *ex parte* property injunction (preventing the sale of assets) and serve a copy of that injunction on the keeper of any marital assets.

Canceling the Credit Cards

A credit card should be viewed as a potential asset. No doubt, once it is used, that asset transforms into a liability for which you may be responsible, in whole or in part.

Before filing for divorce, take possession of every credit card that is either a joint credit card or which has your name on it. Destroy those credit cards, inform the credit card company not to issue any replacement cards (specifically to your spouse), close the account, and begin paying off balance due.

If the credit card company balks at closing the account without your spouse's consent, be insistent; if that fails, advise the credit card company (in writing, by certified mail, return receipt requested) that you will no longer be responsible for any obligation of your spouse on that account after the date of your correspondence. You should not have to pay off the balance due in order to close a credit card account. Be firm and insist on your rights.Keep a copy of your letter to the credit card company and return receipt card.

Ounce of Prevention, Pound of Cure

Withdraw all joint assets (such as bank accounts, brokerage accounts, safety deposit boxes, or the like), immediately before filing for a divorce and place those assets in your name alone. This assumes, that you (acting alone) have the authority to withdraw such assets without the co-signature of your spouse. Redeposit all assets in your sole name in a different brokerage house or different bank. Don't spend the assets, but merely protect and preserve them. If you don't protect assets, your spouse may spend them.

There are a variety of assets that may have liquid value, including life insurance policies, annuities, individual retirement accounts (IRAs), tax sheltered savings plans and annuities, and more. Consult with your attorney on each of these assets and take precautions to protect them. A stitch in time saves nine.

Most divorce parties lack the moral fortitude to take unilateral action and protect their assets. They fear doing anything that may "upset their spouse." Of course, those timid people are upset after the assets have been wasted by their spouse. Then, it requires thousands of dollars in legal fees to rescue these assets. Better to take a unilateral action early on, then to endure the heartache and expense of lost assets later.

Stealing the Family Jewels

It is vital to protect the family records. The family financial documents become important. Tax returns (going back ten years) and the most recent statement of account for every bank, brokerage house, savings, or other financial account are critical. The most recent account statement indicates the account number and location of the asset. That account information provides a lead which may indicate

171

assets that have been wasted or hidden.

Before filing for a divorce, secure all of the family records (dealing with finances, assets, and liabilities) in a safe place where your spouse cannot destroy or tamper with them. If that's a problem then, little by little, remove these assets from the home or business one day at a time, photocopy them, and return the originals. At least then, you construct a duplicate set of family records. This keeps everyone honest and dissuades either spouse from hiding assets or "forgetting" they exist.

Threatening the "IRS Audit"

Sometimes, it is necessary to gain some leverage to negotiate a fair divorce property settlement. It can sometimes be achieved by unsheathing the ultimate weapon: threatening an IRS audit.

Of course, the threat of an IRS audit is a two-edged sword: first, you must be the innocent spouse (who has never signed a tax return, knowing about understated income, overstated expenses, or unearned credits claimed); second, you must be able to prove your innocence; third, your spouse must have committed some tax fraud usually within the last three to seven years. Tax fraud may include understating income, overstating expenses, or claiming credits to which one is not entitled.

The IRS offers rewards of 15% for the amount of taxes collected when a tip is received about tax fraud. If your spouse is being unreasonable, and is guilty of tax misbehavior, your threat of "phoning the IRS" may be enough to bring your spouse back to the bargaining table in a good faith attempt to fairly resolve disputes.

Keep in mind, this is a weapon more effective when threatened than once actively used. Once you actually tip off the IRS, you have spent your ammunition and your gun is empty.

Undressing the Secret Lover

As with tattling to the IRS, you may be able to return your spouse to the bargaining table by exercising your First Amendment freedom of speech about some marital infidelity. By then, you have no concern with infidelity because the divorce is in process. Your spouse should be concerned about any involvement with someone else who was and is still married.

However, it is unlawful to engage in criminal extortion. It would be a crime to threaten something unless you were paid money or received something of value. The threat of tattling about a secret lover to the spouse of such miscreant should only be used in an attempt to bring a spouse back to the bargaining table to talk realistically about what would be a fair and just property settlement.

These are explosive devices which tend to self-detonate. Only professionals should play with explosives. Let your lawyer do the talking.

Deluge of Discovery

One legitimate lever which can be used during divorce proceedings to gain some advantage is the deluge of discovery.

Discovery is a process to seek information by subpoenas, deposition testimony, interrogatories, demands for documents, and requests for a site visit. This entire process of collecting information is generically referred to as *discovery*.

To perpetrate a deluge of discovery that makes your spouse (or their attorney) run around in circles at great expense, you must be able to pay the price (e.g., attorney fees) for such forays. To generate discovery requests, monitor them, collect up such information, synthesize it, and make use of it requires substantial money.

There can also be some embarrassment and humiliation associated with discovery. During the course of most divorces, the issue of fault becomes tangled with property division. A course of discovery may be designed to prove that your spouse was "at fault" for the breakdown of the marriage relationship.

Imagine your spouse's discomfort at deposition testimony (sworn statements made aloud in response to questions and answers before a court reporter). You might request depositions of your spouse's boss, subordinates, co-workers, or others to establish some marital infidelity at work. You might seek similar depositions from members of your spouse's family, church or other similar associations. You might pursue depositions of neighbors or "the boys" or "the girls" with whom your spouse cavorts. People who have traveled with your spouse out of town may offer interesting episodes you can exploit to leverage a fair property settlement.

While discovery costs substantial dollars, if your spouse is reluctant to come to the bargaining table to discuss a fair split of substantial assets, the deluge of discovery may be enough to erode such reluctance.

Who Gets the Etchings?

You know that the divorce is done when everyone decides who gets the etchings. Or it could be the microwave oven (you remember: the extra one, in the garage, on the shelf, you've been saving just in case. . . of divorce?).

The big issues must be solved before the little issues can be discussed. In the end, you must comb the house and, item by item, determine who gets what. To leave this unresolved and to your spouse's discretion (because you don't want to get into a brawl over "petty items") is to purchase trouble. In the end, every little thing will have to be allocated.

The Bankruptcy Option

If you must pay money to your spouse because of a bad result of a property settlement, there is little you can do about it. The only recourse to extricating yourself from a bad property settlement is to be insolvent and then declare bankruptcy.

If you don't have the cash due on a property settlement, and if your spouse has taken no collateral or security in any property to assure that you pay, then you may be uncollectible.

If you cannot afford to be burdened with the property settlement, you may wish to consider playing "the bankruptcy card." There are two chapters of The Bankruptcy Code available: Chapter 13 (which allows you to develop a pay-off plan over a three year period); or, Chapter 7 (which allows you to liquidate all of your assets and use the proceeds to pay off debts, erasing the debts which cannot be paid in full).

Under a Chapter 7 (liquidation) bankruptcy, all of the non-exempt assets in your name are sold. All of your creditors can make claims for their fair share of the assets. The net proceeds from the sale of your assets are divided pro rata among your creditors. While neither alimony nor child support are debts that can be eliminated, a lump sum or time-payment property settlement can be wiped out.

Under a Chapter 13 (reorganization) bankruptcy, you develop a plan to pay off all creditors over three years. Under such an arrangement, whatever extra cash you generate during the three year plan is paid to your creditors proportionally. After the three year plan ends, remaining debts are eliminated.

While the stigma of Chapter 13 (reorganization) is less stinging than that of Chapter 7 (liquidation) bankruptcy, both of them have a substantial negative impact on your future creditworthiness. Nonetheless, if obliged under a property settlement to pay cash over time, and your spouse has no collateral, bankruptcy may present an option.

chapter 10 SPECIAL ASSETS

Marital Assets

Divorce courts consider two types of assets: marital and personal. *Marital assets* are divided by the divorce judge. *Personal assets* are not divided and, instead, are retained by whomever owns those personal assets. The debate, however, is about what constituted *personal* versus *marital* assets.

To oversimplify, any asset that was acquired during the marriage is rebuttably presumed to be part of the marital estate. A "rebuttable presumption" is one which can be overturned by evidence to the contrary. For example, let us consider an inheritance.

You receive an inheritance from a Great Aunt whom you not have seen for years (and for whom you provided no support while alive): that inheritance is normally considered personal property. However, such an inheritance could be a marital asset if your Great Aunt lived in the marital home during her last 10 years and for whome you provided financial support. An inheritance could either be a marital asset or a personal asset, depending on what your Great Aunt intended.

A good divorce lawyer will examine each asset titled solely in the name of one spouse to determine if that asset is either totally personal, totally marital, or a little bit of each.

•••••••••••••••••••••••••••••••••••

The *net value* is the important to consideration you decide whether or not you want an asset, or you wish your spouse to take that asset. When making up the "Yours, Mine & Ours" List, calculate the net values of assets, not merely gross sales values. Let's view an example of a balance sheet approach for dividing marital assets at their net value.

ASSET / LIABILITY	TOTAL	HUSBAND	WIFE
HUSBAND'S CAR	$7,500		
Less Loan	($3,500)		
		$4,000	
WIFE'S CAR	$6,500		
Less Loan	($1,500)		
			$5,000
MARITAL HOME	$125,000		
Commission	($8,750)		
Costs of Sale	($500)		
Less Mortgage	($25,000)		
Less Equity Loan	($1,500)		
			$89,250
I.R.A.		$6,000	$4,000
PENSION		$85,000	
LIFE INSURANCE	$23,000		
Less Loan	($2,300)		
		$20,700	
CREDIT CARDS		($1,500)	
C H A R G E ACCOUNTS			($750)
SUBTOTAL		$114,200	$97,500
CASH TO WIFE		($8,350)	$8,350
TOTAL		$105,850	$105,850

The net value is what an asset is worth after it is sold, after the liens or mortgages have been paid off, and after paying all taxes due because of the sale. If you want an asset, write down the net value (not the gross sales value) of that asset in your column. The best example is the marital home. It is not worth the sales price. From the amount received at sale, you deduce real estate commissions, points, cost of title insurance, mortgage, home equity loans, and more. Whatever is left over after all those items are paid for is the net value of the home.

Therefore, understand that an asset should only be valued at its net worth to you *after sale.*

Slicing the Pension Pie

Common, special assets are the present value of a pension, an individual retirement account (IRA), a tax sheltered annuity, or some other benefit to be paid in the future.

The pension is normally divided by using an order of the divorce court entitled a "Qualified Domestic Relations Order" (QDRO). If a couple has been married during the entire time a pension was accruing, a QDRO instructs the pension plan administrator to pay out two separate checks, one to each spouse.

The amount of each check is determined by making up a mathematical fraction: the top number of the fraction (numerator) is the years of marriage and the bottom number of the fraction (denominator) is the years the pensioner has participated in that retirement plan. So, in a divorce occurring after 5 years of marriage, where the pensioner participated in the retirement plan for 20 years, 5/20th or 1/4 of the pension was accrued during the marriage. Therefore, the non-pensioner spouse is entitled to one-half of 5/20ths of the pension (or 1/8 of the pension) earned until the date of the divorce.

In many divorces, there are only two major assets: a marital home and pension. Assuming the net value of both assets to be roughly equal, the pensioner gets the retirement plan while the non-pensioner is awarded the home and mortgage.

Actuaries are hired to value pensions. The actuary computes the present cash value of the pension using generally accepted actuarial assumptions. This gives a dollar figure to be used during property settlement negotiations.

Remember, a pension is a very valuable asset. Reduced to its present value, the average pension is worth tens of thousands of dollars. The pension usually is not the sole property of the pension plan participant — the one who supposedly *earned* it. Both spouses earned that part of the pension which accrued during the marriage. The portion earned is to be divided as a marital asset.

Valuing the Family Business

Valuing the family business which is operating as an ongoing concern is a difficult task. Closely-held or privately-owned businesses which are not publicly traded at a stock exchange or over-the-counter are most valuable when sold as a going concern.

There are myriad methods for valuing a service business. Some business evaluators will multiply the gross annual earnings by some factor (of 3 or 5 or 7). Other valuation approaches start off with an earnings multiple, then add on the net value of equipment, furniture, fixtures, land and buildings. Whatever method is used, a professional business evaluation expert needs to be employed regardless of whether you want to keep the business or seek a property settlement including your fair share of the value of the business which increased during the marriage.

As with pensions, most courts take a snap-shot approach. Calculate the value of the business at the time of the divorce; subtract the business value on the date of marriage. The difference is the value of the business accrued during the marriage. That accrued value is a marital asset, subject to being divided.

Another factor of valuation considers future cash flow. This is particularly important in a family business which both spouses have labored mightily to build up. That business, had there been no divorce, would have generated a cash flow in future years. This future income stream (in the forms of profits, salaries, and "personal expenses" which constitute business deductions) can be reduced to its present value.

Present value is an important concept, with any asset that is not liquid today (such as pensions, annuities, business interests). The present value concept is this: what cash investment today, at present interest rates, would produce enough principal and interest over the years to match the cash flow of the business, or the pension, or the annuity? The amount of the cash investment required equals the *present value of the future sum*. This present value is a marital asset which can be divided in a divorce.

Family business valuation is complex and is often intensely litigated. Frequently, the marriage which involves a family business as an asset results in the type of divorce which goes to trial. If so, hire expert witnesses, including actuaries and certified public accountants (CPA), to assist is such valuations.

Divorce is a Taxable Event

The tax bite of a divorce can be ferocious. You don't need a dog catcher, but you do need a tax lawyer or CPA to fend off that tax bite. There can be tax consequences in dividing marital property.

Candidly, most divorce specialists do not consider themselves tax law experts. Don't be misled into believing that just because taxes are enacted by law, and lawyers study law, that all attorneys understand tax law. Few do and most will admit it. While tax law intertwines with divorce law, do not assume that every divorce lawyer is a tax specialist. What's a taxpayer to do?

Importantly, discuss with your attorney the potential tax consequences of each separate and distinct paragraph in a divorce judgment. If you attorney suggests getting a tax specialist involved. . . just do it.

Engage in some candid discussion with your legal counselor about the level of tax advice you need. If your attorney feels more comfortable recommending a CPA — particularly one who professes some expertise in the transfer of marital assets — then accept your lawyer's good advice. Remember, you get what you pay for; if you need a CPA and don't hire one, don't complain if you get bitten by the tax dog.

Separate or Joint Tax Returns

The tax issue that troubles parties during a divorce that carries over from one year to the next is — whether to file jointly and how to allocate the refund or taxes due.

Filing status is an important issue while still married, but the divorce is pending. Tax law determines who can file a joint return as a married person. If you are married for any single day during a tax year, you're eligible to file a joint return as a married couple (provided you are not divorced at all during that year). The converse is true: if you are divorced from your spouse, even if the divorce judgment is dated December 31st, you cannot file a joint return with that spouse in that calendar year.

Favorable tax rates are offered to married couples filing jointly. For example, if a married couple filing separately made $41,075 (adjusted gross income), they would pay $1,200 more in taxes by filing separately rather than jointly. It is usually in the best interest of married couples, during the course of a divorce, to work together and file a joint return and divide that return.

Filing jointly is recommended, but only after you calculate your taxes both ways — jointly and separately. If a joint return is to your advantage (and it usually is), then you and your spouse need to discuss two issues: first, whether or not to file jointly; second, how to split the refund or taxes due. File jointly, but only if your spouse has no tax problems. Avoid filing a joint return if your spouse has understated income, overstated expenses, or claimed credits not available.

File separately if your spouse disagrees with your definition of a fair split of the refund. If the children live with you, claim them as dependents and file as "head of household" if you qualify. If you are the non-custodial parent, claim the children as dependents and, if your spouse did not work, claim your spouse as a dependent as well. During a divorce, the spouse who gets the dependents is governed by the ancient rule, "First in time, first in right." First one to file their tax return wins.

Splitting the refund or taxes due should be agreed upon in advance. A split could be equal or divided in proportion to gross income or taxes withheld. Any arrangement is acceptable, provided there is an agreement in writing, approved by your divorce attorneys. If an agreement can be reached, there can be substantial tax savings in filing joint return; compared to the status of "married filing separately," a joint return will almost always mean a larger refund or a smaller amount of taxes due. This is because the tax rate is lowest for couples who are "married filing jointly."

Dividing the refund check can be a problem. When a divorce is filed, mutual trust is crippled. The most effective way is for both spouses to take the refund check to the bank; endorse the tax refund check in front of the teller, asking for two separate checks in return — one to each spouse in the agreed amount.

The *"innocent spouse rule"* should determine if you file a joint return when married. As a spouse, you can be liable for your mate's failure pay required taxes unless, as the innocent spouse, you had no reason to know of the omission of income or the inflation of deductions or credits. The IRS considers all circumstances in deciding when to hold the innocent spouse liable for the tax period. The IRS considers the extent to which the "innocent" spouse benefitted from the tax underpayment in deciding this "equity" issue.

If you suspect your spouse has been less than honest with the IRS, you lose the status of being an innocent spouse. Your spouse's tax fraud might include:

- failing to claim all gross income realized,

- exaggerating the amount of deductions,

- claiming credits not otherwise available.

If your spouse is suspect of tax fraud, then file a separate return. If you know too much, you can't be an "innocent spouse." Avoid filing a joint tax return if your spouse understates income, inflates deductions, or claims unavailable credits.

Avoiding Tax Consequences

How you liquidate and dispose of assets in the course of a divorce proceeding can have important tax consequences. For example, assume the husband keeps the marital home; in exchange, the wife keeps certain individual retirement accounts (IRA) equal to one-half the net value of the home. Depending on exactly how that IRA transfer occurs, the husband could be liable for taxes on the IRA, or the wife could get the tax bite, instead.

A husband pays taxes if he first withdraws the IRA from the bank and gives a check for the amount of the IRA withdrawal to his soon-to-be ex-wife. At the end of the tax year, the husband will owe taxes for the amount of the IRA plus early withdrawal penalties.

A wife pays taxes, however, if the husband merely transfers the IRA to the wife, pursuant to an order contained in the divorce judgment. An IRA transfer pursuant to a divorce judgment is a non-taxable event. Thus, it is a transfer with no tax consequences to the husband. Indeed, if the wife then withdraws the IRA after the divorce judgment, but prior to retirement, then she will owe taxes for the amount of the IRA plus early withdrawal penalties.

Whenever you transfer or receive assets as a result of a divorce judgment, learn about the tax consequences to you in advance. Not all transfers of assets in a divorce have tax consequences.

No income taxes are usually due upon the transfer of a titled vehicle (such as a car, boat, snowmobile) from one spouse to another. However, stocks and bonds are a different story.

When capital assets (stocks and bonds, property, coins, etc.) are transferred from one spouse to another, the *basis* of those assets is transferred as well. If you get the asset, you pay the taxes (if any, associated with that asset). With capital assets such as stocks and bonds, capital gains tax must be paid (if the value has increased since purchase); you may also take a tax deduction if there has been a capital loss (when the value has fallen since acquisition).

The transfer of a family business may have tax consequences. Some businesses lose money. When they do lose money, their net operating loss may be carried forward. A loss carryover (especially one which can reduce your personal taxes) is an important tax advantage.

A loss carryover shelters this year's income from taxes. Each $1.00 of loss wipes out $1.00 of income, leaving no taxes due on

$1.00. When considering the transfer of a business interest, calculate how much of that net operating loss carryover you can use to your tax benefit.

One way or the other, there is either a tax benefit or a tax burden to every asset. Get advice from a CPA or tax attorney and. . . don't leave home without it.

•••••••••••••••••••••••••••••••••

Glenn and Norma had several business interests. One such business had been losing money (on paper only) for years (because of a net operating loss carryover).

In the divorce property settlement, Glenn generously gave his wife several income-producing assets and he kept the remaining assets. On paper, it looked like a 50/50 split. However, Glenn kept one business for his own. It had shown a loss every year for the past five years. This was due to a operating loss a few years previously which could be carried forward for 15 years, until it was used up by profits.

Glenn generously offered to take responsibility for this failing business enterprise. His wife, of course, wanted nothing to do with an unprofitable and "failing" asset. She surrendered the losing enterprise to Glenn; she took nothing in exchange.

Glenn was able to successfully use the loss carryover from this failing business to shelter the income-producing properties that he received in the property settlement. While Norma obtained income-producing properties, all of her income was taxable, yet Glenn's income-producing properties were totally sheltered from taxes because of the loss carryover.

Moral of the Story
Look a gift horse in the mouth. Be careful when your spouse

too willingly agrees to take an asset which, on its face, seems to have little value and to be more trouble than it's worth. Be sure you check with both your attorney and CPA to see if that asset might have some tax value that does not appear on its face.

Keeping an Inheritance

The mere fact that you've inherited some property during the course of your marriage does not necessarily mean that property is yours and will remain yours alone even after a divorce. To keep your inheritance, you must prove it is personal property and must have avoided commingling it with marital assets.

Distinguish whether an inheritance was meant to be yours alone or whether it was a marital bequest to both spouses. Of course, inheritances come into your possession by one of two means: you are either given some property from the estate of the deceased person and the property is titled in your name, or you are a common or joint tenant on financial account which reverts to you with your other tenant passes away.

Normally, property is inherited from one's relatives, commonly a parent or grandparent. The property inherited by you alone is considered personal property (unless there were some unique circumstances bringing that property into the marital estate).

For example, if your mother has lived in your marital home for many years, with both spouses caring for mother, or you have lent your mother money (which was marital assets), then an inheritance from mother might be considered a "marital asset." In this example, both spouses together might be considered to have "earned" the inheritance. Then, such an inheritance would be considered marital property.

Once you receive a separate, personal inheritance, however, what you do next is important. To preserve a personal inheritance as sole and separate property, you must not commingle it with your other marital assets. If such an inheritance is personal, and if the assets are liquid (such as bank account, brokerage account, or the like), keep those assets in your name alone and place your social security number on the account.

If the inherited property is represented by some title or document (certificate of deposit, title to a vehicle or boat, deed for real property, etc.), then continue to maintain that property titled in your name alone. If the inherited property is personal in nature (coins, jewelry, collections), then you should preserve these assets in a place over which you have sole and separate control (such as a safety deposit box in your name alone).

Inherited property can become part of the marital estate when you commingle it with marital assets. For example, if you inherit some antique furniture and you place it in your common, marital dining room where it is used for many years by the entire family, that property may be considered marital property. Or you may inherit $10,000 which you deposit into a joint bank account with your spouse. Both of you freely deposit into and withdraw from that account for any marital purpose, from groceries to graduation gifts. The interest earned on that bank account is reported on your joint tax return. No doubt, what began as a personal inheritance has become, over time, a marital asset. The inheritance has lost its unique and separate character.

Under such an example, the inheritance is no longer "personal property" but, rather, becomes "marital property." Once an inheritance becomes "marital property," it may be divided by the divorce court as part of a divorce property settlement.

To be sure that you maintain an inheritance as your own, keep that inheritance separate from marital property and titled in your name alone. If there are any taxes due (such as interest income earned), then withdraw enough money from that inheritance account, deposit only the amount necessary to pay the taxes in the joint account, and pay the taxes from that joint account. Only by such separate steps can you maintain an inheritance as your own.

Visiting the Vacation Bank

Another special asset is accrued paid leave time (such as vacation pay, personal leave, business days, and sick leave). Occasionally, this paid time can be converted to cash. Then, its cash value is a marital asset, subject to division.

Be sure to include in the marital estate any cash value for accrued paid leave time for which your spouse may be entitled. Such paid leave time arguably is part of the marital estate.

Cash for College

Another special asset is the cost of a college diploma or advanced professional degree acquired with marital assets while married. Such a degree may be a "marital asset" if acquired with marital funds and at the expense of the marriage relationship, though one party will enjoy the benefit of such degree.

What is the value of a college or professional degree acquired during the marriage? The worth of such an asset should be the present value of all of the monies which were invested to acquire that degree. Instead of being spent on the degree, these marital assets could have been deposited into an interest bearing account paying a reasonable return on investment. Consider the cost of tuition, books, lab fees, parking, meals on campus, and the like.

The value of a college degree should not be ignored as a marital asset, in favor of a request of alimony. Nonetheless, if the college degree has allowed one spouse to open a business or begin a professional practice, the value of this advanced education might be considered a divorce asset.

The Lawsuit Settlement

A personal injury settlement paid to one spouse for injuries occurring during the marriage may be the personal (not marital) property of the injured spouse. As with an inheritance, the proceeds of a personal injury settlement must be kept as sole and separate property to preserve its unique nature as "personal property."

To commingle a personal injury settlement with marital assets may be to convert those funds into a marital asset. Of course, marital assets are divided by divorce courts, while "personal property" is not part of the marital estate and is not divisible.

If you are the recipient of a personal injury settlement, place that settlement in a sole and separate bank account, make sure your social security number alone is on that bank account, and withdraw whatever is necessary annually to pay taxes on the interest income. Only the amount withdrawn to pay taxes should be commingled with other marital assets if filing a joint income tax return.

Season Tickets

Season tickets may have been in your family for years; yet, these special event passes can be marital assets. If you like the event, there is only one other reason to purchase season tickets: location, location, location.

The valuation of season tickets to a special event (ball game, symphony, concert, ballet, theater) is not merely the face value but, rather, the replacement cost for similarly situated seats on the open (read "scalper") market. Where there is no "open market" for such season tickets, you may not be able to obtain substitute tickets. Surrender the season tickets only upon an exchange of fair value. More than the face value, for sure.

In squabbles over such special assets as season tickets, the judge may threaten to rule with the wisdom of Solomon: if you can't agree on who gets the season tickets, then each of you will be given one ticket and you may sit next to each other for the next 20 years. A reasonable alternative is to give each party one-half of the pairs of tickets.

Another valuation method is to let one person place a monetary value on the asset while letting the other person choose whether, at that price, to keep the tickets or take the cash. That is the old, "You cut the pie; I pick the first piece" trick. For example, if a husband has $500 worth of ballet tickets, he might value these at $1,500; for that price, the wife can either pay the price and keep the tickets, or surrender the tickets and get paid $1,500. Choose who plays which role by the flip of a coin. Such a wise approach compels reasonableness.

The Club Membership

A special asset which burdens but a few in life is the exclusive club membership. Your family may have purchased a membership in a private, members-only tennis club, athletic club, yacht club, hunt club, golf club, or the like. A club membership acquired during marriage may have cost a pretty penny as an initiation fee.

The initiation fee may be a marital asset, as well as the right to retain and continue the club membership. If you do not wish to retain the club membership after the divorce, or cannot afford to do so, be sure your spouse exchanges fair consideration in the amount of one-half of the value of the club membership.

The club membership is at least worth one-half of the initiation fee calculated as of when originally paid. If one spouse gets the membership, and the deprived spouse wishes to join that same club, perhaps, the value should be one-half of the present initiation fee. No doubt, a club membership has value both to the recipient as well as to the spouse who sacrifices such membership and is part of the marital estate.

Fishing for Marital Assets

Marital assets are divided up in a divorce while *personal assets* remain the property of their original owner. These are words that trip from the tongue of a divorce lawyer, but are much more difficult to define. With every asset, you must consider whether it is personal or part of the marital estate. Some assets may be hybrid, that is some part may be personal, while the remainder may derive from the marital estate.

This list helps you begin thinking about what assets may need to be allocated in a divorce judgment.

☐ Gather every possibly-helpful document.

☐ Request basic financial documents from your spouse.

☐ File formal written interrogatories, after reviewing basic financial documents.

☐ Successive series of written interrogatories following review of initial interrogatory answers (which may be i incomplete, vague or evasive).

☐ Deposition upon oral examination.
  - Opposite party on financial matters and on conduct of the parties.
  - Persons having personal knowledge of financial matters.
  - Expert witnesses for the opposite party (i.e., psychiatrist, psychologist, social worker, family doctor,

CPA, marriage counselor, etc.).
- Client's expert witnesses.
- Witnesses to the misconduct of the parties.

☐ Motion/Subpoena for Production for Documents.
- Inspection of premises, both home and business relevant to divorce proceedings. Photograph property within the home.
- Physical and Mental Examination of Persons.
- Demand for Admissions.
- Video Depositions.

Property — Sources of Income

☐ Original and amended versions of all tax returns and schedules (personal, corporate, partnership, and others) since marriage; copies of all audits pertaining to such returns.

☐ Weekly pay stubs for past two years.

☐ Tax free income.

☐ Tax shelters, annuities, savings plans.

☐ Business ventures.

☐ Real estate.

☐ Wages.

☐ Annuity plan income.

☐ Deferred income plans, Section 401(k) Plans.

☐ Dividends.

☐ Interest.

☐ Worker's Disability Compensation (WDC).

☐ Aid to Families of Dependent Children (AFDC).

☐ Veteran's benefits.

☐ Social Security Income (SSI).

☐ Independent contractor fees.

☐ Pension, annuity and profit sharing programs.

☐ Retirement and pension plan income.

☐ Individual Retirement Accounts (IRA).

☐ Simplified Employee Pensions (SEP).

☐ Property rental.

☐ Trust funds.

☐ Land contracts.

☐ Insurance.

☐ Unemployment Compensation (UC).

☐ Supplemental Unemployment Benefits (SUB).

☐ Long term disability insurance (LTD).

☐ Accidental death and dismemberment (AD & D) insurance.

☐ Sickness and accident (S & A) and disability insurance.

☐ Stock saving programs.

☐ Inheritances.

☐ Other income sources.

Property — Assets

☐ Cash on hand.

☐ Interests in real estate (whether individually, as tenant-in-common, joint tenants, or tenant-by-entireties), present and future, purchasing or owned, including the location, value, balance due, payments.

☐ Lottery (foreign and domestic) tickets and winnings.

☐ Security interests or liens.

☐ Bank deposits, personal and business.
- Passbooks, daily interest.
- Type, account number, date of balance, signatories.
- Review and copying of check registers and canceled checks.
- Review and copying of savings passbooks.

☐ Certificates of deposit (CD).

☐ Accounts with credit unions.

☐ Bank time certificates.

☐ Short and long term obligations.
- Corporate bonds.
- Savings bonds.
- Treasury notes.

☐ Chose in action, pending, contingent, settled.
- List all legal actions during marriage, including bankruptcy.

☐ Trusts in which opposite party is a settlor.

☐ Personal property.
- Art objects.
- Collections (coin, stamp).
- Household goods.
- Marital home.
- Vacation property.
- Automobiles, boats, campers, airplanes, motorcycles, snowmobiles, trailers, mobile homes.
- Jewelry.
- Antiques.
- Photography equipment.

☐ Patents, inventions, copyrights.

☐ Rights of inheritance.
- History of property inherited during marriage.
- Sources, value and conversion to present form.
- Rights of inheritance.
- Rights of future inheritance, vested or contingent.

☐ Securities (stocks, bonds).
- Review of IRS Schedule D and intangibles tax returns since marriage.
- Review and copying of brokerage accounts.
- Inventory of all safe deposit boxes in whatever state.

☐ Business interests.
- Partnerships, limited and general.
- Corporations (IRS 1120 and 1120S returns).
- Joint ventures.
- Sole proprietorships (IRS Schedule C).
- All assumed names on file with county or state.

☐ Prior financial statements issued by opposite party.
- Loan applications to banks, SBA, Small Business Investment Corporation, Minority Enterprise Small Business Investment Corporations, and other potential financiers.
- Previous litigation.

☐ Life insurance.
- Production and examination of policies.

- Determination of cash values and encumbrances.
- Government life insurance.

☐ All applications for credit cards, lines-of-credits, and other loans.

☐ Health and hospital-medical-surgical (HMS) insurance.

☐ Death benefits.

☐ Pension plans, employer funded, Keogh plans, other retirement plans.

☐ Accounts receivable.
  - Professional fees.
  - Intrafamily.
  - Tax refunds.
  - All outstanding loans and "bad debts," regardless of age.

☐ Employment contracts (independent contractor or employee), deferred income rights.

☐ Leasehold interests in apartments, co-ops, condominiums.

☐ Charge accounts, personal, family use, and business use.
  - Access by third party.
  - Monthly charge statements.

☐ Other assets.

Property—Liabilities

- ☐ Sole.

- ☐ Joint.

- ☐ Contingent.

chapter 11 ALIMONY

The Sore That Never Heals

While most states theoretically permit alimony to be awarded to either spouse, some states only permit alimony awards in favor of the wife. This gender bias has led some to view alimony as a punitive measure (if you are the payor). Others view alimony as the scrap of bread tossed from among the leftovers at the wedding feast (if you are the recipient). Whatever your perspective, alimony means acrimony.

Upon every divorce from the bonds of matrimony or legal separation (called a divorce "from bed and board"), the court may award alimony from the assets accumulated during the marriage. Some courts, instead of alimony, require to payor to pay specific expenses (mortgage, utilities, taxes, insurance, transportation). Other courts, rather than deal with the specifics, prefer a lump sum award of alimony designed to provide for the necessaries of life, including:

- Household expenses (such as mortgage, utilities, taxes, insurance, repairs).
- Transportation (car payments, insurance, repairs).
- Food, clothing, haircuts, laundry, and miscellaneous.

- Health care (physician, dental, optical).

- Other reasonable expenses necessary to maintain the *status quo*.

If you don't wish to pay alimony, there are two people you must convince: the judge and your spouse. Only when both the judge and your spouse believe that you should not pay alimony will you be free of potential liability.

The courts routinely are confronted with requests for two types of alimony: temporary alimony and permanent alimony.

Opening Round: Temporary Alimony

The first sign there will be an alimony fight is indicated by reading the divorce complaint. If you spouse seeks alimony, the fine print will say so. The second indication of a fight over alimony is if your spouse seeks temporary alimony, that is, alimony paid weekly or monthly while the divorce is pending.

Temporary alimony allows the recipient to maintain a financial *status quo* until the marital property can be allocated in a final judgment. Since contested divorces often progress over 24 to 36 months, a request or motion for temporary alimony is often made.

Alimony helps maintain the recipient spouse in the fashion to which that spouse has become accustomed. Alimony helps maintain the *status quo*. For example, a working husband (whose wife dedicated herself to the family household) might make periodic alimony payments sufficient for her to maintain the household, her mode of transportation, and pre-divorce life style. Such alimony helps maintain the economic *status quo* until the divorce court can assess the marital estate and determine a division of assets.

A motion for temporary alimony puts the potential payor at an immediate disadvantage. The hearing is usually scheduled quickly. Such an immediate hearing can catch a potential alimony payor off guard. If you are the one at a disadvantage, move for an adjournment of the hearing on temporary alimony so you can hire an attorney. If you have an attorney, move for an adjournment so that you can be prepared to discuss the two issues (the recipient's need and your ability to pay).

Never agree to temporary alimony just because the amount is small. Little boxes contain big surprises. What begins as a nominal amount of alimony has a tendency to mushroom quickly and never go away. Never agree to temporary alimony to placate an angry spouse. The idea is flawed because temporary alimony is akin to providing the enemy with the weapons to wage a long campaign against you.

At a hearing on temporary alimony, the court will examine these issues:

- Does the potential recipient need alimony to maintain the *status quo*? If not, then no alimony is awarded; if so, then. . .

- How much alimony does the potential recipient need to maintain their living standard while the divorce is pending?

- Can the potential alimony payor afford to pay the alimony which the court has determined is needed? If not, then no alimony is paid; if so, then the court will compute the potential payor's income and may include "everything under the sun" when defining "income."

Why Pay Alimony?

Alimony is paid for one or many reasons. The court considers all relevant factors in determining whether alimony is necessary and, if so, how much alimony is needed. Most courts will consider some or all of these factors:

- *Personal factors* (including age, health, physical and emotional conditions).

- *Income sources* (from retirement plans, social security).

- *Marital situation* (including duration of marriage, marital standard of living).

- *Personal background* (including education, vocational skills, time required to acquire sufficient further education or training which would enable future gainful employment).

- *Ability to pay* (including all assets and liabilities).

- *Personal net worth* (including financial resources, expectations, family inheritances, property brought to the marriage which the court allows to be taken from the marriage).

- *Contribution to marriage* (including services in homemaking, child care, education, and career building of the other spouse).

- *Earning potential* (including employability, occupation, respective duties as custodians of minor children born of the marriage).

- *Fault* (including cause of divorce, economic mis conduct, merit, adultery and the circumstances).

- *Tax consequences* of accepting certain property as part of a property settlement (which property might be diminished by the payment of taxes).

- *Need* of recipient for support.

- *Other relevant factors* necessary to do equity and justice between the parties (including character of the case, all circumstances of the parties, justice and equity).

All of these factors and more will be considered by a court in determining whether or not one should pay alimony. However, the court does not automatically award alimony without first asking a series of questions of the potentially alimony recipient:

> *Fault* Are you free of any substantial blame or fault in causing the breakdown of the marriage? If "yes," then. . .

> *Need* Do you really need alimony to maintain your standard of living? If "yes," then. . .

> *Income* Are you without any other sources of income from which you can draw, and is there no property you can sell, to provide for your needs? If "yes," then. . .

Duration How long do you need to receive alimony before your can retrain yourself to become reemployable? And. . .

Amount How much alimony must you have to maintain your standard of living in the meantime?

Whether alimony is to be temporary or permanent, this assessment must be made regarding the potential alimony recipient.

Friend of the Court

Before alimony is granted, increased, or decreased, many courts will seek an investigation and recommendation from the Friend of the Court (FOC). The FOC will examine the alimony needs of the potential recipient and examine the payor's ability to pay. All other relevant factors will be considered.

Customarily, the FOC will issue a written recommendation whether or not alimony should be awarded; if so, whether the alimony is temporary or permanent; the amount of the alimony; the time period for which alimony should be paid.

Uncle Sam Helps Pay Alimony

You may wish to pay alimony because alimony may have favorable tax consequences. Indeed, how alimony is structured determines those tax consequences. As a general rule, unless the divorce judgment says otherwise, most alimony payments are considered tax deductible to the payor; likewise, the same payments are taxable income for the alimony recipient. This tax treatment pertains to alimony or separate maintenance payments that are:

✓ Received by a spouse (or on behalf of the spouse) under a divorce or separation instrument; and,

✓ The divorce or separation instrument is silent about whether the payments are deductible to the payor, and the payments are income to the recipient; and,

✓ The recipient and the payor live in different households while the payments are made; and,

✓ The alimony obligation ends upon the recipient's death; and,

✓ After the recipient's death, the divorce judgment does not require the payor to start making some substitute payments (in cash or property); after the recipient's death, alimony or separate maintenance payments must be terminated.

When all of these conditions are met, alimony is tax deductible to the payor and taxable to the payee. However, if *any one of these criteria is missing*, instead, alimony would then be tax deductible to the recipient and taxable to the payor.

For example, let us assume that a divorce decree states that $100 per week of alimony is payable for 10 years; assume further that the divorce decree requires alimony to continue for the 10 year period, even if the recipient dies during that decade. In that instance, one criterion is missing and the payor would not be able to consider alimony as tax deductible and the recipient would not pay taxes on the alimony received.

Alimony has subtle tax consequences. Though it may be called *alimony*, it's not necessarily tax deductible to the payor and not automatically income to the recipient.

COLA is not a Soft Drink

Some alimony provisions call for a cost-of-living allowance (COLA). This gives alimony an automatic escalator clause over time.

A COLA is inserted into an alimony clause to avoid the attorney fees and inconvenience of periodically returning to court to consider alimony modifications. A COLA provision is usually directly tied to a percentage increase in the monthly Bureau of Labor Statistics Consumer Price Index (BLS-CPI). In theory, the CPI could mean alimony increases (when the cost-of-living rises) or decreases (when the cost-of-living falls). That's the theory; however, the reality is that the cost-of-living rarely, if ever, falls.

With a COLA provision, the changing needs of the recipient and the ability of the payor to afford more alimony, are unrelated to the amount of alimony that will actually be paid. A COLA provision is a formula approach. A COLA provision which limits alimony increases to the periodic increases in the BLS-CPA is:

- *Good for the payor* where the alimony recipient's need for alimony rises faster than does the cost-of-living;

- *Bad for the payor* where, over time, the recipient gets additional income (such as pensions, annuities, inheritances) but alimony is not reduced accordingly.

- *Good for the recipient* where the alimony recipient's need for money decreases over time while the cost-of-living rises during the same period;

- *Bad for the recipient* where, over time, the need for money increases dramatically (due to illness, need

> for skilled nursing care, requirement to move) but the cost-of-living rises only slowly.

The Rule of Thumb here is that an alimony recipient should seek a COLA provision, while the payor should resist a COLA clause with equal force.

Alimony is *Permanent Press*

In most places, the court can order either temporary or permanent alimony. Some courts restrict permanent alimony to disabled spouses. Alimony can be a permanent obligation when so ordered by the court. The duration of alimony usually is left to the discretion of the court.

Permanent alimony is most likely ordered in marriages longer than 15 years, particularly where one spouse had not worked outside the home and has devoted all efforts to nurturing and raising a family. Because alimony can be a "forever thing," it is important to do what you can to mitigate your expose to permanent alimony.

The alimony payment may be a lump sum payment (called "alimony in gross") or might be paid in smaller sums from time to time (called "periodic alimony").

Even in "no fault" divorce states, the fault of the payor spouse (and the comparative innocence of the recipient spouse) can be a factor in deciding how much alimony, if any, to award.

A key factor to consider in awarding permanent alimony is the value of the marital estate awarded to the potential alimony recipient. If the property settlement is sufficient to otherwise support the proposed alimony recipient, then no alimony need be awarded.

Assume a $750,000 marital estate consisting totally of funds deposited in a money market account; upon a 50/50 split, each divorcing party would receive $375,000. Many courts would consider that additional alimony is unnecessary under that example. No doubt, few divorcing couples could boast such a respectable nest egg.

The only defense against permanent alimony is to be sure that your spouse does not need alimony to continue living in the manner to which you both are accustomed. That requires pre-planning which can be a substantial cost-saver in the event of divorce. Translation for a male-dominated society: if you keep her barefooted, pregnant, and staked to the kitchen floor (while you are busy nurturing your professional career), expect to pay for such servitude with permanent alimony.

Alimony can be a never-ending obligation. Even the most modest of alimony payment plans has serious cost implications: alimony at $100 per week for 20 years means spending more than $100,000 over two decades — and that doesn't include any increases.

Rather than becoming obligated for periodic alimony, do a little horse trading. Offer a bigger share of the property settlement rather than succumb to alimony. This is effective for most people: cash today is more psychologically attractive than a mere promise to pay tomorrow.

When a marriage of 15 years or more ends in divorce, the termination of that union is rarely sudden. Both spouses begin to sense the erosion of the relationship over time. If you find yourself in such a situation, knowing that a long-term marriage may ultimately end, and you do nothing to change the course of current affairs, then consider the issue of permanent alimony.

Alimony is awarded because a recipient spouse has no independent means of support. Certain doors have permanently closed behind the potential alimony recipient who has invested in the marriage, family, and household over the years. The best prevention to paying permanent alimony is to assure that your spouse has a wealth of job skills and education. Only this will assure your spouse's independence and prevent the scorpion sting of permanent alimony.

Urge your spouse to return to school, to earn that undergraduate or graduate degree, to obtain the licensure or certification which improves employability. Nurture your spouse to find other interests outside the home which interests may convert to gainful employment. Only an independent means of support will guarantee your freedom from the permanent press of alimony.

Permanent alimony can be paid after the divorce is final. Such permanent alimony can be modifiable or non-modifiable. If non-modifiable, permanent alimony is a guaranteed lump sum payment, or is guaranteed to be made over a period of months or years, regardless. If modifiable, permanent alimony can be discontinued when a particular event occurs.

Events that can trigger termination of permanent, modifiable alimony may include the recipient's: remarriage; cohabitation with an unrelated male; the passage of a specified number of months or years; or, death. Permanent alimony can be considered supportive or rehabilitative.

Retraining Allowance

One form of post-judgment alimony is rehabilitative. This type of alimony is paid for a limited period of months or years after the final divorce. This temporary payment period allows the recipient spouse to rehabilitate work skills needed to find gainful employment.

For example, assume a physician is married to a business school graduate. The disparity of incomes is pronounced. The physician may pay rehabilitative alimony over two years allowing the business school graduate to return to graduate school to earn a Master of Business Degree (MBA). This version of alimony may be considered a *vocational retraining allowance.* If you also pay child care costs of young children while your *ex-* obtains this retraining, this may be termed a *nursery fee arrangement.*

In another example, assume a certified public accountant (CPA) who, during the marriage, finished college and earned an MBA in graduate school. The CPA is divorcing from a spouse who is a licensed practical nurse (LPN) with only an associate degree from a community college. The LPN's certification has lapsed because the LPN stayed home to raise a family. The court might order this CPA to pay rehabilitative alimony for up to five years, allowing the LPN to return to college and earn a Masters Degree in Nursing. This rehabilitates and educationally elevates the LPN to a plane equivalent to that of the CPA who had earned an MBA while married.

Rehabilitative alimony is usually geared to allow the homemaker spouse to gain needed skills to be economically self-sufficient, thus, avoiding the need for permanent alimony. Where appropriate, the court will consider whether alimony is necessary from a permanent standpoint (because the recipient spouse can never be gainfully employed).

If Not Now, Then When?

Every divorce judgment should recite specific language memorializing the judge's ruling on alimony. A divorce judgment that is silent on alimony can cause serious problems in the future. The divorce judgment should stated whether: alimony is granted; permanently denied; denied now, but subject to review if circumstances change. The court which has not forever barred the door to alimony may reconsider that issue periodically.

Alimony can be awarded even after a divorce judgment has been granted in some states unless the issue of alimony is specifically addressed in the divorce judgment and the court has said that alimony is permanently closed. A well-crafted divorce judgment will contain explicit language about how alimony is to be treated after the divorce is effective.

If alimony is denied in a divorce judgment, then the judgment usually states whether denial is permanent or whether alimony can be revisited at a later date. Of course, if you are the potential payor of alimony, you will want a divorce judgment to state that the issue of alimony is resolved by denying alimony and by permanently closing that issue forever. Conversely, if you are the potential alimony recipient, you would like the divorce judgment to indicate that the issue of alimony is not permanently closed and may be revisited at a later date.

Enforcing Alimony Awards

To enforce alimony awards, the judge can issue an order for the reluctant alimony payor to show cause why the payor should not be held in contempt of court for failing to pay the full alimony or to do so on time. The payor who refuses to timely pay alimony when ordered by the court may be jailed for contempt of court. Such imprisonment is evidence that *Debtor's Prison* is alive and well in America.

The payor who has an ability to pay, but refuses or neglects to do so, can be jailed. In theory, the alimony payor who can afford to pay holds the "keys to the jail cell" in their own pocket. When able to do so, only by paying an amount toward reducing the alimony arrearage can payor be set free.

Modification of Alimony Awards

After a divorce judgment is rendered, the court may modify alimony by increasing or decreasing the amount to be paid. The court balances the need of the alimony recipient against the payor's ability to pay.

Decreases in alimony can be made in favor of the payor if there is a material or substantially reduced ability to pay, regardless of the need of alimony recipient; this is under the ancient, equitable principle which says, "You can't squeeze blood from a stone."

Increases in alimony can be made in favor of the recipient if there is a change in circumstances and the recipient demonstrates a legitimate need for more funds while the payor has the corresponding ability to pay.

Before alimony is modified after a judgement of divorce, the exact language of a divorce judgment must be read carefully. Some awards of alimony in a divorce judgment are non-modifiable. That is, they can neither be increased nor decreased. Other divorce judgements contain automatic trigger which terminate alimony (such as upon the recipient's remarriage or cohabiting with an unrelated male). If alimony is modifiable, the court will consider:

- The recipient's remarriage.
- Increase or decrease in the alimony recipient's needs for money.
- Increase or decrease in the ability of the payor to afford more alimony.

Generally speaking, the remarriage of the payor is irrelevant. Once alimony is awarded, the recipient's claim is entitled to primacy. Some courts operate under the premise that if the payor cannot afford to provide for two spouses, then the payor should not remarry.

Tax Tricks that Backfired

Brandon thought himself quite clever with divorce and taxes. There were children. Brandon persuaded Janelle, his wife, that Brandon should only pay $5.00 per week in child support (because it was not tax deductible). Instead, Brandon wanted to pay all of the real "child support" money in the form of alimony (which would be tax deductible to Brandon). Brandon told his attorney about this and Janelle silently consented to this arrangement. The judge agreed to the arrangement and a consent judgment of divorce was signed.

Because Brandon was a highly paid executive, he was in the top income tax rate. Normally, he would be required to pay $400 per week in child support, none of which would be tax deductible. However, by allocating virtually all "child support" instead to alimony, the "alimony" payments became deductible to Brandon and became income to his ex-wife.

Brandon could afford to pay as much as $600 per month in alimony which (after taxes) had the same impact as if he were paying $400 per month in child support. Since Janelle stayed at home with the children, her income tax rate was rock bottom. Janelle would pay the income taxes (but at a lower rate than Brandon). This "alimony" scheme also provided more money for Brandon's children who could enjoy a better lifestyle. This was all well and good. . . while it lasted.

When the consent judgment of divorce was signed, Brandon made specific statement on the record before the court reporter about his unique alimony arrangement. The judgment itself was silent about this arrangement, for obvious tax reasons.

The first two years went by and Janelle religiously cashed her weekly $600 check. After 24 months, however, Janelle wanted more money, so she could remain at home with the children. By then, the original divorce judge had been promoted to the court of appeals and was no longer assigned to their divorce case.

Two years having passed, Janelle hired a new lawyer (who had no knowledge of the private deal made between Brandon and Janelle). Janelle's new attorney filed a motion to increase child support. The new judge was appalled that child support had originally been set so low, at a mere $5.00 per child per week.

Janelle feigned no knowledge of any "deal" with Brandon about paying less child support and more alimony. The court record equally was silent about any such agreement. Nothing had been put in writing and Janelle's lawyer was ignorant of any "handshake deal."

The court increased the child support, also ordering that Janelle's $600 monthly "alimony" continue as well. Brandon was now required to pay $600 per month of alimony and an additional $600 per month of child support. Brandon's cleverly disguised alimony had fallen like a house of cards.

Moral of the Story
There is more than one way to skin a cat, particularly when it's somebody else's tiger and not yours. Be careful when playing fast and loose with the tax code. Just because you say its "alimony" doesn't mean its "child support."

Playing the Bankruptcy Card

Accepting a promise to pay, instead of alimony, can be risk business. That promise to pay may be considered part of the property settlement, instead of the alimony obligation it really is. Property settlements are debts dischargeable in bankruptcy; alimony cannot be discharged in bankruptcy court.

A husband may take the marital home and, instead of paying alimony, may offer to pay the wife $50,000 over five years; here, the wife should take a mortgage in the marital home as security for the promise of a future $50,000 payment. That home mortgage should be properly recorded. Without a recorded mortgage, the promise to pay may be just a property settlement obligation dischargeable in bankruptcy.

Donald and Dorothy had been married for a quarter of a century before being divorced. They had acquired a marital home but it was heavily mortgaged with both a first mortgage and a home equity loan.

During the divorce, Donald wanted to keep the marital home; however, he would also pay off the mortgage and home equity loans. Donald would "hold Dorothy harmless" from these obligations and she would not be required to pay them.

Rather than award Dorothy alimony, the property settlement required Donald to pay several lump sum payments of $10,000 each year for five years. Dorothy got no security to guarantee these payments. Dorothy was also given these lump sum payments, while Donald got the parties' remaining personal property. These lump sum payments were specifically listed as being part of the property settlement, not lump sum alimony. This became an important distinction later.

Now the distinction which became important here is that alimony is not a debt that can be discharged in bankruptcy. On the other hand, property settlements can be eliminated by filing bankruptcy. Thus, as the time approached for Donald to make his first lump sum payment, market prices for the home he had been awarded began to fall. Donald could not secure an additional mortgage to pay the first $10,000 payment to Dorothy.

There was a soft real estate market, mortgage rates remained high, selling prices dropped significantly, as did home values, all because of a recession. The marital home that once had a substantial equity had now plummeted in worth. So, Donald had a marital home that was encumbered by two mortgages. Unable to make Dorothy's first lump sum payment of $10,000 Donald filed for bankruptcy in a Chapter 7 proceeding.

Under the law of the state where Donald resided, as a debtor in bankruptcy, he was allowed a "homestead exemption" of $9,500. In other words, Donald was allowed to keep his home if the net value was no more than $9,500.

After paying off the two mortgages, Donald demonstrated to the bankruptcy court that his home equity was worth under $9,500. The disastrously low real estate value for this home was in Donald's favor. The bankruptcy court discharged the five lump sum property settlement payments of $10,000 each; Donald kept the home.

After bankruptcy, Dorothy lost her property settlement and Donald kept the home subject to the first mortgage and the home equity loan. In time, real estate values improved, Donald sold the home, made a tidy profit and was lawfully able to keep the proceeds as his own.

Moral of the Story
Alimony is not dischargeable in bankruptcy. Be sure that any alimony award in the divorce judgment is clearly specified as such. The failure to clearly designate certain payments as lump sum alimony award may qualify those payments are nothing more than part of a "property settlement." Property settlements can be discharged in bankruptcy, while alimony cannot.

Marrying Off Your *Ex-*

When it comes to modifying alimony, the fact that your ex-spouse has or has not remarried after divorcing you is irrelevant. . . unless, of course, you are the payor.

The alimony provisions of most divorce judgments treat spousal support as a quasi-permanent arrangement. Conceptually, alimony is a support payment made while an ex-spouse is not other-wise able to provide for their own necessaries in life. Alimony is a two-sided coin with the need the recipient on one side and ability to the payor to afford alimony on the other. Thus, if the need of the alimony recipient decreases, for example, due to remarriage, then the support can be reduced or terminated.

One strategy to permanently terminate modifiable alimony would be to marry off your *ex-*. Of course, before engaging in such Machiavellian manipulations, be sure that remarriage alone will permanently terminate your alimony obligation. Also, be sure that your alimony obligation will not be rekindled if that remarriage should result in divorce.

•••••••••••••••••••••••••••••••••

Cindy was a popular "rock star" who had married Bruce early in her singing career. Though Cindy had been a professional entertainer for 10 years, Cindy was still less than 30 years old; nonetheless, her marriage to Bruce had lasted more than a decade before the divorce.

Cindy tired of Bruce who had been her unpaid manager. As her manager, however, Bruce demonstrated to the divorce court that it was his business skills that had catapulted Cindy to fame. The divorce judge awarded Bruce alimony of $5,000 per month. Because Bruce was young (himself under age 30), the alimony was considered semi-permanent until Bruce otherwise become gainfully employed or remarried.

Bruce claimed that his skills of promoting and managing a rock star were difficult to market elsewhere. Stars are not as easy to come by as are managers. For all intents and purposes, Bruce settled into semi-retirement at this early age. Provided he did not remarry, Bruce could stroke this alimony "goose who laid the golden egg."

It became clear to Cindy that her alimony obligation to Bruce (at the rate of $60,000 per year, subject to periodic increases for cost-of-living adjustments) could continue forever. Cindy made a decisive move. She found a fledgling female vocalist who could benefit from Bruce's promotion and managerial skills. Cindy promised to be the mentor of her professional singing career only if she would marry Bruce — just long enough to kill that alimony albatross hanging around Cindy's neck.

While Bruce would not readily surrender his $60,000 per year in alimony for a young, impoverished singer, Cindy helped this young woman to culture an image of being independently wealthy. After a makeover, this candidate appeared like she didn't *need* to sing for her supper, but *wanted* to croon a tune just for fun.

The young singer had a total "makeover" not only of her singing skills and professional appearance but, also, of her *apparent* financial status. She not only appeared to have talent and great potential, but she also seemed to have a fat bank account. At least, that was what Bruce believed.

This new flame in Bruce's life not only needed Bruce's managerial and promotional skills but, also, she presented ever greater financial possibilities than did his meager $5,000 per month alimony check. Bank-rolled by Cindy behind the scenes, this up and coming star, even if she stumbled, apparently could support Bruce's life as one of the rich and famous.

Bruce took the bait and after a passionate and whirlwind romance, took the leap and married Cindy's protégée. Cindy quickly terminated the alimony and moved for a modification of the divorce judgment to permanently end her alimony obligation. All the while, Bruce's new, young wife was treating him to a spectacular around-the-world vacation, lavishing him with comforts and gifts that only the wealthy could afford. Convinced that he had died and gone to heaven, Bruce did not oppose Cindy's modification of the divorce judgment and readily agreed to terminate alimony permanently.

With the divorce judgment modification in hand, Cindy saved

herself $5,000 per month and acquired a new singing talent which she herself could manage professionally — Bruce's soon-to-be ex-wife.

Upon returning from their around-the-world glitzy vacation, Bruce's new singing wife filed for divorce. Stunned by the fact that he had sacrificed his alimony only to remarry, Bruce sought an annulment from his new wife. An unsympathetic divorce judge scolded Bruce saying, "You made your own bed; now you can sleep in it."

Moral of the Story
To marry off your *ex-* may permanently discharge your alimony obligation. Your former spouse's new marital bliss can forgive your permanent alimony obligation.